TABLE OF CONTENTS

Editor
Gene Myers

Designer
Tracee Hamilton

Coordinator
Dave Robinson

Photo editor
Marcia Prouse

Copy editors
*Bill Collison
Owen Davis
Brad Betker
Reid Creager
Bob Ellis
Free Press sports copy desk*

Researchers
*Janie Reilly
Angelo Veneri*

Special thanks
*Diane Bond
Ed Duffy
John Goecke*

Front cover
Craig Porter

Back cover
William DeKay

Front cover: Joe Dumars, Bill Laimbeer, Mark Aguirre admired the hardware.

Back cover: John Salley received a hero's welcome.

Right: Dumars raised his game to new heights.

INTRODUCTION

By Mitch Albom

Love, they say, can be better the second time around. Basketball is another story. The second time around, as NBA champions, means night after night of opposing teams wanting a piece of you. It means fans who scream when you drop two in a row. It means reporters saying "They're not the same" and critics saying "They miss so and so." It means spotlights and question marks and a season that seems to take forever and it means pressure, the kind that makes your head throb. *Are we still good? Will we still wear the crown? Is somebody gaining on us?*

What was it then, that the Pistons must have felt the night of June 14, 1990, when, with one second left on the clock, Vinnie Johnson rose from the hardwood, cocked the ball behind his head, and let fly a jump shot over the outstretched arm of Portland's Jerome Kersey? What was going through their minds as that ball flew toward that basket? John Salley buried his face in a towel. "I couldn't watch," he would say. Chuck Daly swallowed a lump in his throat. Joe Dumars and Isiah Thomas and Dennis Rodman were frozen on the court, lost in the moment . . . only their eyes were moving, tracking the path of the ball as . . . it . . . fell . . . through . . . the . . .

. . . net.

Good!

The Pistons couldn't be touched on the court. Isiah Thomas reached out and touched plenty of people when the Pistons returned from Portland with their second NBA championship.

Twice as nice. Twice as sweet. Twice as satisfying. That's what they felt. "This one was for us," Bill Laimbeer would say, champagne pouring down his face, as they celebrated what they'd waited for all season, the second crown.

"Yeah!" gushed a dripping Mark Aguirre. "We're part of history."

You know what? They are. All of them. The big guys, such as James Edwards, the Buddha Train, and John Salley, all smiles and blocked shots, and Rodman, the human jumping bean and Laimbeer, Mr. Irritation. The bench guys: Aguirre, who found a home in relief shooting, and Johnson, the Microwave, who waited his whole career for his most historic basket. And, of course, the little guys, the Palace Guards, Thomas and Dumars, whose penetration through the lane was like taking a machete through vines and whose outside shooting brought stars down from the skies. They led the way. The smallest ones. To the biggest Detroit sports story in years.

Back-to-back champions. Only the third franchise ever to do it. They endured tragedy, injury, shooting slumps and self-doubts. They still came out as the best in the world. It was a hell of a story, really, something that, like the championship itself, might be even better the second time around. Or the third. Or the fourth.

Turn the page and see for yourself . . . ■

THE SUMMER

Joe Dumars and Isiah Thomas were the toast of the town after the Pistons swept the Lakers in June 1989 for their first NBA championship.

JOY AND SORROW

By Mitch Albom

Just a moment ago, he was dancing. Just a moment ago, he was spraying champagne on his teammates, laughing with those gap-teeth, shaking his big, burly body and singing *"BAAAD BOYS! BAAAD BOYS!"* Just a moment ago, Rick Mahorn was the muscle around the heart of the Pistons' first NBA championship team.

And now he is gone.

So much for fantasy. Welcome back to real life. On the day of the Pistons' 1989 championship parade, their love dance with the city of Detroit, their management rolled the dice and lost: Mahorn was left unprotected in the expansion draft — which for some ridiculous reason is held

before the hangovers wear off from the NBA Finals — and the Minnesota Timberwolves, a team that doesn't even have uniforms yet, plucked the baddest of the Bad Boys right off the shelf. "It's . . . a business deal," said a crushed Mahorn as he tried to drive away from the Palace celebration on this June 15 afternoon, amid throngs of people who were cheering and waving banners, not even aware that their hero had just been stolen. Mahorn looked away. He had his hands on the wheel and a bag of souvenirs on the seat and he was trying not to cry in front of a TV camera and this was wrong, all wrong. It doesn't matter how mean and nasty his reputation; it doesn't matter if his back injury makes him questionable. He had just touched the end of the rainbow, the dream of every kid who ever laced up a basketball sneaker. All this — the cheers, the parade, the glory — was paradise.

And he was being thrown out.

Shouldn't there be a moratorium on this kind of news? Shouldn't we be able to celebrate for one solid day, for 24 hours, without some poke in the ribs from the real world? Instead, this. Farewell, Rickey. Just a moment ago, he was on the podium in front of a delirious crowd, leading them in a Bad Boys cheer. He walked over to coach Chuck Daly, shook his hand, and said, "Thank you for having faith in me." He walked over to general manager Jack McCloskey, grabbed his hand and said, "Thanks for sticking with me through my weight problem." He was the Bad Boy turned good, the thug in the movies who, in the final scene, reveals his tender side. And gets shot in the heart.

"It's a sad, sad day," McCloskey said. "We feel like we're being penalized for having depth." He shook his head. He tried to explain. He said he had been on the phone all morning and afternoon — even on the parade float — trying to work out a deal to keep the Timberwolves from taking Mahorn. But it was his decision to leave Mahorn unprotected in the first place, and there is no way to minimize the impact. It was like throwing tear gas at a wedding.

Why Rickey? The starting power forward? McCloskey said his bad back was part of the reason. But there is more to a player than his anatomy. What about his heart? On the court, Mahorn was the symbol of Pistons toughness. You did not mess with him, and you did not mess with this team.

The Pistons knew they would have to leave a

good player unprotected (each team could protect eight), in order to preserve the likes of Dennis Rodman, John Salley and the starters. Vinnie Johnson's playoff performance almost guaranteed his protection. So many thought the one to go would be James Edwards, the backup center. No knock on Edwards, a wonderful player and a class guy, but he would turn 34 during the 1989-90 season (Mahorn only 31), he would make $800,000 a year (as opposed to Mahorn's $600,000) and he was mostly effective off the bench. An expansion team looking for starters, leaders and affordable salaries might be more likely to pass on Edwards. Hey. The whole thing is a gamble. You try to offer guys the expansion teams won't take. But Mahorn? A veteran? A starter? An outspoken leader in the locker room?

He was gone like ice cream on a hot afternoon.

He was a symbol of what the right team can do for the wrong guy. He arrived four years ago, fat, unhappy, traded from Washington. He did not want to be in Detroit. That first season he kept to himself, and fans wondered whether the Pistons had picked up a flabby, mean-looking mistake. But

Rick Mahorn led the Palace cheers, and his teammates showed off their hardware — unaware that moments earlier Minnesota had taken Mahorn in the expansion draft. He was the No. 2 pick — after Orlando chose Knicks forward Sidney Green, a former Piston.

teammates. They'll get you. And the fellow Pistons got to Mahorn, implored him to play harder, convinced him he was needed, but that he had to pull his share. He lost weight, he improved his defense, he signed on for the long haul. And he became a player. Now, before they even put the ring on his finger, he was gone. The news jolted the Pistons in mid-celebration. They entered their locker room drunk with glee, the whole city loved them, and this was the best. And they emerged, minutes later, as if there had been a death in the family. Which, in a way, there was.

Perhaps, in time, this will be seen as an unavoidable business move. Why Rickey? Why now? Why must a harmless, wonderful day of celebration take a shot to the stomach? Just a moment ago, he was on the Palace podium, microphone in hand, leading the crowd in a chorus of *"BAAAD BOYS!"* Suddenly, to everyone's delight, he leaned over and kissed each of his teammates, one at a time, cheek to cheek. The toughest, roughest Piston? Cheek to cheek?

How sad. He had no idea he was kissing them all good-bye. ∎

BAD BOYS OF SUMMER

By Gene Myers

The Summer of '89. It was the shortest in Pistons' history. And it was the sweetest.

■ **JUNE 13:** Shortly before midnight Detroit time, the Pistons finish a four-game sweep of the Lakers with a 105-97 victory in California. The Bad Boys have won their first NBA championship.

■ **JUNE 15:** The Pistons' day-long title celebration ends sadly when starting power forward Rick Mahorn is lost to the Minnesota Timberwolves in the expansion draft.

■ **JUNE 20:** President George Bush receives the Pistons in Washington. Captain Isiah Thomas, citing the loss of Mahorn, declares the end of the "Bad Boys" era. The entire team, including Mahorn, makes the trip, except rookie Michael Williams, recovering from hernia surgery. Bush says the Pistons' charitable contributions contradicted their ruffian reputation in the NBA: "You are known as the Bad Boys on the court, but your off-the-court activities definitely showed a kinder and gentler side to the Pistons." . . . The Detroit Free Press publishes *Bad Boys* — the first book about the championship season.

■ **JUNE 22:** Playoffs MVP Joe Dumars, who shuns the spotlight, stops in glittery New York long enough to receive his trophy and a Jeep Cherokee. . . . Chief executive officer Tom Wilson reveals that the Pistons, despite selling out every game, will raise ticket prices.

■ **JUNE 27:** With the 27th — and last — pick in the first round, the Pistons draft Illinois forward Kenny Battle, then trade his rights and guard Michael Williams to Phoenix for the rights to Arizona forward Anthony Cook, selected by the Suns with the 24th pick. The Pistons hope Cook, although only 6-feet-9 and 215 pounds, will help fill the bulk void created by Mahorn's departure.

■ **JUNE 30:** With Bad Boys no longer the Pistons' nickname, the Free Press asks its readers to pick a new one. From the 1,338 entries, coach Chuck Daly selects The Daly Double, submitted by Jackie Crow of Farmington Hills, Mich. The other finalists: Bold Boys, Broom Brothers, Crunch Bunch, Disassemblyline, Liquidators, Mowdowners, Repeat Offenders, Smother Brothers and Unstoppables. Among the

most bizarre: Backstabbers, Batmen and Rodman, Changed Gang, Daly Routeam, Gazebos, Generic Boys, Isiah and the Peacemakers, Naughty Children, New Bad Boys, Not-So-Bad Boys and Zeke 'N Da Streak.

■ **JULY 2:** John Long, about to turn 33, becomes an unrestricted free agent. The Pistons, looking for younger guards, decide not to re-sign him.

■ **JULY 3:** When Joe Dumars won the MVP award, he announced in a TV commercial that he was going to Disney World. With his fiancee, Dumars finally gets there.

■ **JULY 7:** Isiah Thomas watches in Grand Rapids as the presses roll off the first copies of his 256-page hardcover book, *Bad Boys! An Inside Look at the Detroit Pistons 1988-89 Season.*

■ **JULY 10:** The Pistons' new video, *Motor City Madness,* debuts in the Palace to underwhelming reviews; the Free Press scores it 4 out of 10.

■ **JULY 15:** Joe Dumars signs a contract for $8

After scaling the basketball summit, Captain Thomas met President Bush.

looks heavy and sluggish competing in the Sandy Sanders summer league at Eastern Michigan.

■ **SEPT. 1:** The Pistons lose two prospects. Anthony Cook, their first-round draft acquisition, signs with the Paok team in Greece. He reportedly will receive $250,000 from Paok; with extras such as a car, an apartment and other bonuses, the total package could approach $350,000. And Jon Koncak holds a press conference to explain why he will stay in Atlanta, thanks to a six-year, $13.2 million contract from the Hawks. Koncak never would have gotten that deal without the Pistons' $2.5 million offer sheet.

■ **SEPT. 9:** About 1,400 people, including many of the groom's teammates and many of the bride's second-grade students, pack Immaculate Conception Cathedral in Lake Charles, La., to see Joe Dumars marry his college sweetheart, Debbie Marie Nelson. Said Dumars' mother, Ophelia: "It looked like most of the team got in in time for the bachelor party."

■ **OCT. 3:** After the Lakers refuse to offer a multi-year contract, David Greenwood, a 32-year-old free-agent power forward, signs for one year with the Pistons.

■ **OCT. 6:** Training camp opens at the University of Windsor. William Bedford dons a Pistons uniform for the first time in 18 months, changing from No. 25 to 00 to "represent a fresh start."

■ **OCT. 11:** The Pistons waive Daren Queenan, CBA rookie of the year and one-time leading fourth-guard candidate. Also cut are rookie guards Monroe Douglass and Roland Gray.

■ **OCT. 27:** Minnesota trades holdout Rick Mahorn to Philadelphia for three draft picks — a first-rounder in 1991 and two second-rounders in 1992. Mahorn, meanwhile, ends talks with an Italian team, Glaxo Verona.

■ **OCT. 29:** Unable to swing a trade, the Pistons waive second-year small forward Fennis Dembo, their 12th man in 1988-89.

■ **OCT. 30:** Philadelphia's Charles Barkley and Rick Mahorn don't suit up, but the Pistons and 76ers nonetheless brawl during an exhibition game before 25,007 at Toronto's SkyDome. The main event features James Edwards against Mike Gminski, with Isiah Thomas as the third man in; all are ejected and later fined.

■ **NOV. 1:** In their final cuts, the Pistons waive rookies Reggie Fox, a Baldwin, Mich., native who played guard for Wyoming, and Mark Hughes, a Muskegon Reeths-Puffer forward who played at Michigan. The 12th roster spot goes to Stan Kimbrough, a rookie guard from Xavier (Ohio).

■ **NOV. 3:** The Pistons start pursuit of their second straight NBA championship with four new players — Stan Kimbrough, William Bedford, Scott Hastings and David Greenwood. ■

million spanning six years, making him the second-highest-paid Piston behind Isiah Thomas, who makes $2 million annually. "I'm happy, I'm happy," Dumars says from his home in Natchitoches, La. . . . The Pistons also sign 6-10 free agent — and free spirit — Scott Hastings, a seven-year veteran coming off a so-so season with the expansion Miami Heat.

■ **AUG. 11:** At Isiah Thomas' Summer Classic, Rick Mahorn suits up for the Pistons for the final time. The fans bid an emotional farewell.

■ **AUG. 17:** The Pistons stun the NBA by offering a one-year, $2.5 million contract to Atlanta backup center Jon Koncak. The Hawks have 15 days to match the offer or Koncak, who averaged 4.7 points and 6.1 rebounds, becomes the highest-paid Piston. . . . Pistons center William Bedford, who missed the entire 1988-89 season because of drug rehabilitation, plays his first public basketball game in 16 months. He

THE REUNION

By Corky Meinecke

The party lived.

Isiah Thomas' Summer Classic, played Aug. 11 before a near-capacity crowd at the Palace, was a rousing success, even if the participants were both out of shape and a bit rusty. Thousands of dollars were raised for Detroit's public high school programs — $240,000, to be exact — and Pistons fans said their final good-bye to power forward Rick Mahorn, who was drafted two months earlier by the expansion Minnesota Timberwolves.

There was the usual assortment of alley-oop dunks and no-look passes and three-point bombs, but the highlight of the evening was the pre-game introduction of Mahorn. He was greeted by a standing ovation and the Bad Boys cheer he made popular during the Pistons' championship season. At that point, Mahorn shed his tough-guy image. "It was tough to hold back the tears," he said. "But I managed to. It's hard. I had become a part of a family, a special family. And now it's over with. I'm going to miss it. I really am."

The Pistons, with Mahorn for the last time, edged a collection of NBA all-stars, 184-181. The evening ended with an impromptu dunk session led by Atlanta forward Dominique Wilkins, who scored a game-high 54 points. After a myriad of dunks, Lakers guard Magic Johnson grabbed the microphone and asked the fans to give Mahorn "a great send-off."

And they did. "I didn't expect this," Mahorn said, "but it feels great." As for the game, he said: "At least we held them to under 200 points."

Thomas assembled eight of his teammates, plus new addition Scott Hastings and free agent Mark Hughes, a starting forward on Michigan's 1989 NCAA championship team. Missing were Bill Laimbeer, James Edwards, Fennis Dembo and Michael Williams, who was traded to Phoenix in the draft-day deal for Arizona's Anthony Cook.

Each summer Thomas, like many NBA big names, stages an all-star game. A few days before his, Thomas played with Mark Aguirre and John Salley in Johnson's California benefit — and the Pistons were constantly booed by Lakers fans. Thomas used his game to help Dave Bing's drive to pay for fall sports at Detroit's 23 public high schools; the athletic programs had been canceled after a failed millage election. "I've always been the guy to deliver the biggest check," Thomas

It was Isiah's party, but Rick Mahorn could cry if he wanted to.

said on the eve of his game. "And this time will be no different." Bing, the former Piston and owner of Bing Steel in Detroit, eventually raised $300,000 — all but $60,000 from Thomas' benefit — and fall sports were reinstated.

Pistons guard Joe Dumars picked up where he left off in the NBA Finals, hitting his first two jumpers. He suited up eight pounds lighter than he was for Game 4 of the finals. Eight pounds lighter? Wasn't he MVP of the playoffs? Wasn't he rewarded with a new contract in July? "I wanted to come back in tip-top condition," Dumars said. "One of my goals has been to come back each year lighter than I was the year before."

Dumars' schedule had been less hectic than immediately after the finals — "I'm working out four hours a day, so that takes up most of my time," he said — but he still couldn't go anywhere, in Michigan or at his home in Louisiana, without causing a commotion. Being a regular Joe, he said, was "out the window now."

And so went Isiah's Summer Reunion and Rickey's Fond Farewell. ∎

THE SEASON

The Pistons and
Dennis Rodman
battled Beasts of
the East such as
Philadelphia's
Charles Barkley
in the 82-game
grind known as
the NBA's
regular season.

OPENING CEREMONIES

By Charlie Vincent

The Pistons got it all in their season opener, the best of both worlds.

One more time they celebrated what they did last season — stamped, endorsed and validated the first NBA championship in the history of this old franchise. And then they went out and did something they had not been able to do even once in their most successful season. They beat the New York Knicks, 106-103.

They had not really wanted to mix the two; that's what they said. They feared that the pregame celebration of their championship season would distract from the chore at hand. They would rather have had this ceremony some other time, possibly some other place, and saved all their energy and all their attention for the Knicks. That's what they said until the lights were dimmed on Nov. 3, a fabulous Friday night. And until the music started and the sounds of "We Are the Champions" filled the Palace.

When the spotlights danced through the arena and the video of the 1988-89 season's final game appeared on the large screen above the scoreboard, this bunch of young millionaires cared suddenly — at least for the moment — more about accomplishments than about money. Standing on the court, they could not tear their eyes from the giant images on the screen. "You couldn't help it," Isiah Thomas said. "I was so overcome with emotion. . . . When the ceremony started, it just hits you."

As captain of this team, though, Thomas had to maintain enough composure to say a few words. And he told the capacity crowd what it wanted to hear. "We shared some of the greatest moments together and some of the most painful moments together . . . and we can honestly say we shared them with you," he said, raising the championship trophy over his head. "On behalf of the Detroit Pistons, myself, my family and Joshua (his son), this is for the fans of Detroit." There is a measure of theater in Thomas, a flair for the dramatic. He saluted the fans with the trophy. When David Stern handed him the championship ring, Thomas — noted kisser of Magic Johnson — leaned over and kissed the commissioner on

With Isiah Thomas' help, the Pistons had a banner night ringing in the new season.

the left cheek.

But Thomas had warned owner Bill Davidson a couple of days earlier of possible dramatic consequences from the celebration. "He told me that both times when the Los Angeles Lakers celebrated their championships on opening night, they got blown out," Davidson said. But the man who bought this basketball team when it was a forgotten stepchild in a city wild about hockey, playing in Cobo Arena before a couple of thousand fans, would not allow that piece of history to ruin this night. "Tonight," he said, "is not as good as the night we won the championship. But almost. Almost."

This celebration came with all the trappings. There were the spotlights, the $4,000 championship rings, the NBA championship trophy, and the banner that proclaimed them the best team in all of professional basketball.

Before the night was over, the Pistons had beaten the only team they didn't in 1988-89 — the team that had won all four meetings.

Finally, the new season had begun. And a new quest had begun.

Repeat. ■

ALL-STAR GAME

By Drew Sharp

Chuck Daly was wrong. It *is* possible to actually coach in an All-Star Game.

The Pistons' contribution to the Eastern Conference All-Star team proved to be more than just cosmetic. The All-Stars also inherited the Pistons' defensive mentality, shutting down the Western Conference for a 130-113 victory Feb. 11 in the 40th All-Star Game before a sellout crowd of 14,810 at Miami Arena. The West's output was the lowest since it was on the short end of a 123-109 score in 1976.

Defense isn't expected in All-Star Games, primarily because good team defense requires participants to mesh well and All-Star rosters are usually made up of players who aren't teammates. But eight of the East's 12-man roster came from three teams. The Pistons' Isiah Thomas, Joe Dumars and Dennis Rodman were joined by three Celtics — Larry Bird, Robert Parish and Kevin McHale — and two Chicago Bulls — Michael Jordan and Scottie Pippen. "When you have familiarity like that, it makes it easier to get that cohesiveness you need," said Thomas, who finished with 15 points (on 7-of-12 shooting), nine assists, four rebounds and three steals.

Capitalizing on that advantage, Daly impressed upon his players the importance of defense. "You take those guys from Boston," he said. "They're used to this. You tell them to do something once, and you don't have to tell them twice." Throughout the game, Daly, in his All-Star debut, was heard shouting "Hand up!" and "Help!" which meant to keep a hand in the shooter's face and assist on the double team. "I can't say enough about how well the guys played," Daly said. "I was particularly pleased by the way they worked defensively. You love it when everybody plays well and you win."

It was a strange sight nonetheless. The game was played as though the Pistons were going against Chicago for first place in the Central Division rather than against a collection of the NBA's top scorers. "Chuck told us before the game that he was a defensive coach," McHale said. "And he wanted some help. I'm not used to

Joe Dumars, Isiah Thomas and Magic Johnson were dressed-to-kill, starry-eyed spectators during the dunk competition. Chuck Daly, who pleaded for defense with assistant Brendan Suhr, toyed with wearing a tuxedo but went with his lucky blue suit.

the game that he wanted us to work on defense — the same thing I've heard for five years."

And Rodman said: "We were well represented here, and I think that made all of us especially hungry to get the win."

The East executed as well offensively as on defense, shooting 54 percent from the floor. Led by Jordan's and Barkley's 17 points, the East had seven players in double figures. Magic Johnson, the Michigan Stater from Lansing Everett, was the West's lone bright spot, leading all scorers with 22 points and winning his first Most Valuable Player Award. Johnson received three votes, one

Fast-talking John Salley lost his voice after working 12 hours on an All-Star Weekend TV piece for NBA Entertainment.

hearing something like that during these games. It was refreshing, to say the least."

The West finished with a 43.8 field-goal shooting percentage. Proficient scorers such as the Lakers' James Worthy (1-of-11 shooting) and Houston's Akeem Olajuwon (2-of-14) were neutralized. The crowd responded louder to Rodman's high-flying block of Worthy and the 76ers' Charles Barkley's rejection of Olajuwon than the spectacular dunks and passes.

"This could be the start of a trend," said Rodman, whose selection was criticized for his lack of offensive skills. Rodman had nothing to feel inferior about with all the West's missed free throws (16-of-26) and field goals (46-of-105). "I didn't feel out of place at all," said Rodman, who had four points and four rebounds in 11 minutes. "It felt just like a normal game for me. I'm used to putting forth an effort to play good defense. You might start getting used to seeing more defense in these games. Those days of both teams scoring 140 points may be over."

"It was just like every game I've played in my five years in the league," said Dumars, who had nine points and five assists. "Chuck said before

more than New York's Patrick Ewing, Thomas (a two-time winner), Jordan and Parish.

If there was one letdown for Pistons followers, it was that Dumars, Rodman and Thomas never played together. Rodman played with Thomas and then with Dumars, but Dumars and Thomas were never paired. "I was having so much fun out there that I didn't even realize it," Dumars said. "But I'm not worried about it. We'll get our chance someday." ■

THE HALL OF FAMER

By Charlie Vincent

The Hall of Fame should not be as difficult to get into as heaven, but almost. Most people think it should be enough to merely hit a baseball far and frequently, win a Super Bowl or two, or average 25 points for a long NBA career.

Here's holding out for more.

There should be no charlatans there, no fakers, no marginal players, no crooks, no frauds, nobody whose picture is as likely to show up in a

were a few thousand fans who knew the players and Gus the peanut vendor in the balcony, and each other, on a first-name basis. They filled a few of the voids in Cobo Arena but left empty spaces on those winter nights in the late '60s and early '70s. In his entire Pistons career, about two million people saw Dave Bing play in Detroit — about the same number who saw the Pistons play in the Palace the past two seasons.

Too bad. More people should have seen him and what he could do with a basketball.

post office as in a sports section. Halls of fame should be filled with people like one the basketball hall honored Feb. 8. They should all be filled with people like Dave Bing, who was elected along with Elvin Hayes, Earl (The Pearl) Monroe and the late Neil Johnston.

Before there was an Isiah Thomas, a Joe Dumars, a Dennis Rodman, before there was a Silverdome or a Palace, before there was a single NBA championship banner with Detroit's name emblazoned upon it, there was Dave Bing. And for Detroit basketball fans in those years, there was precious little else.

There was Bob Lanier, of course. And there

Dave Bing was there to lend a hand at Isiah Thomas' summer all-star game, along with another pretty fair guard — Magic Johnson.

He has been retired for 12 seasons — a Detroit businessman and a civic force — but still no Piston has made more free throws than Bing. Only Lanier has scored more points. Bing was a complete player, but what he could do best was shoot. "Without sounding cocky," he said, "I think I deserve it. I've worked for it."

Bing is the only Piston whose number (21) has been retired. He joins Dave DeBusschere and Bob Houbregs — who played only the final 17 games of his career with Detroit — as the only Pistons in the Basketball Hall of Fame.

Other Pistons will be there someday.

But none will deserve it more. ∎

THE 25-1 STREAK

By Drew Sharp

Maybe after the season, the Pistons will look back on their magical 25-1 run through winter, savoring — if only briefly — how they held the league hostage for two months.

Oh, what a ride. The Pistons struck fear in the hearts of the NBA. They were untouchable at the Palace and stalked the road like scavengers looking for their next meal. The 25-1 record was the league's third-best one-loss winning streak ever, and the longest since the Celtics went 25-1 during the 1980-81 season.

"We'll remember it as the time that we came together as a team," forward Dennis Rodman said. "Its size probably won't hit us until long after the season is over. We'll probably read something that's talking about the streak and we'll look up and say, 'Damn, that was pretty impressive, wasn't it?'"

The streak began Jan. 23 with a 107-95 victory in Chicago, the Pistons regaining first place in the Central Division. Two days earlier, the Pistons had lost to the Lakers at the Palace, 107-97. The national TV loss rattled their sense of security. They realized that although they were the defending NBA champs, they weren't the league's best team. Things had to change. Rodman replaced injured Mark Aguirre in the starting lineup. Reserve John Salley played with more consistency. Suddenly, all the parts were working in unison. The Pistons reeled off 13 straight victories, lost at Atlanta and then won 12 in a row. The streak ended with three straight losses in Texas.

The Pistons fell nine victories short of the Lakers' 34-1 record but reserved a place among the great teams in history. "There's no way you can deny that when you consider what they accomplished," said Houston coach Don Chaney. "To have a streak like that today, with all the great scorers, is a tremendous achievement."

During the Pistons' 25-1 stretch, their opponents averaged fewer than 95 points a game and below 44 percent shooting. Only once — in the 112-103 Atlanta loss Feb. 23 — did a team shoot better than 50 percent. Sixteen of the 26 opponents were held to fewer than 100 points, nine under 90 and one (Miami, Feb. 17) under 80. Seven of the eight previous teams to go at least 20-1 during a season won NBA titles.

The Pistons would make it 8-for-9. ∎

The streak started when Dennis Rodman — against his wishes — replaced Mark Aguirre in the starting lineup. In the 26 games, Rodman averaged 30.7 minutes (up 3.9), 10.5 rebounds (up 1.4) and 60.3 percent floor shooting (up 4.3).

THAT CHAMPIONSHIP SEASON

By Gene Myers

Despite plenty of tough times, the Pistons finished 59-23, captured the Central Division and tied for the second-best record in the NBA.

■ **NOV. 7:** Michael Jordan scores 40 points as Chicago hands the Pistons their first loss, 117-114. For scuffling with rookie Stacey King, Pistons newcomer Scott Hastings receives the season's first fine — $1,500, twice King's fine.

■ **NOV. 8:** The Pistons miss 59 shots (31-for-90), score 25 first-half points and lose at Indiana, 95-74. Only in a 81-71 loss in 1988 in Atlanta had Detroit scored fewer points.

■ **NOV. 11:** By blowing an 11-point lead in the fourth quarter, the Pistons lose in Miami, 88-84, and fall to .500 at 3-3.

■ **NOV. 26:** For the 20th straight time, the Pistons lose, 102-82, in Portland, where they had not won since Oct. 19, 1974.

■ **NOV. 27:** With the Pistons only 7-5, Chuck Daly announces that James Edwards will replace John Salley as the starting power forward. The team would win 44 of its next 54 games (.815).

■ **DEC. 1:** The Pistons hold the Lakers scoreless in overtime for a 108-97 victory.

■ **DEC. 6:** Vinnie Johnson snaps a season-long slump with 17 fourth-quarter points and 24 total in a 115-107 victory over Washington.

■ **DEC. 8:** Rick Mahorn scores 22 points, grabs 14 rebounds and knocks down almost everyone in Philadelphia's 107-101 victory.

■ **DEC. 12:** Daly as NBC-TV's top NBA analyst in 1990-91? "I know nothing about that," Daly says. The rumor would last the season.

■ **DEC. 19:** The Pistons end a three-game losing streak, 94-77, over Seattle. In 1988-89, Detroit never lost more than two in a row; its worst stretch was three losses in four January games.

■ **JAN 4:** Sacramento hires a new coach, Dick Motta, the Pistons' TV color commentator.

■ **JAN. 5:** John MacLeod, fired by Dallas early in the season, lost out to Motta for the Kings' job but succeeds Motta on Pistons broadcasts.

■ **JAN. 9:** Holding Jordan to 16 points, the Pistons take first place from the Bulls, 100-90. The most dramatic moment comes when Dennis Rodman flies over the press table chasing a loose ball and clobbers Free Press sports writer Drew Sharp, smashing his computer and scattering beverages, papers and assorted media apparatus. Sharp suffers a nasty bump on his head.

The Pistons surrendered 98.3 points a game — lowest in the league. The expansion Minnesota Timberwolves, at 99.4, were the only other team to give up fewer than 100.

■**JAN. 21:** The Lakers end a seven-game losing streak to the Pistons, 107-97, in the Palace, knocking Detroit out of first place.

■**JAN. 23:** With Aguirre sidelined and flu-ridden Joe Dumars barely able to stand, the Pistons rely on their bench — David Greenwood gets six rebounds, William Bedford eight second-quarter points — to win in Chicago, 107-95. The Pistons, who hold Jordan to 11-for-31 shooting, regain first place, which they never surrender.

■**JAN. 29:** Daly makes the final change in the starting lineup — Rodman replaces Aguirre as the small forward. The Pistons, then 29-14, had won three straight games, all started by Rodman.

■**FEB. 21:** Dumars scores his 5,000th career point in a 140-109 victory over Orlando, the Pistons' 13th straight.

■**FEB. 23:** Host Atlanta beats the Pistons, 112-103, preventing them from tying the longest professional winning streak in Detroit history — 14 games, by the Tigers in 1909 and 1934.

■**FEB. 27:** Houston falls, 106-102, after Rodman, giving away four inches and 40 pounds to center Akeem Olajuwon, forces overtime by deflecting Olajuwon's last-second shot.

■**MARCH 2:** Mahorn receives his championship ring. Actually, Edwards had delivered it to a friend of Mahorn's in Washington in November. The friend had passed the ring to Mahorn. He had passed it to his mother in Hartford, Conn. The ring was retrieved for a thunderous pregame ceremony. With the Pistons down four with 10 seconds left, Thomas drills a three-pointer, steals an inbounds pass and hits a lay-up to force overtime. Detroit wins, 115-112.

■**MARCH 14:** Trainer Mike Abdenour receives six months' probation and a fine for faking an emergency to Auburn Hills' 911 unit. On March 6 — two days after Loyola Marymount's Hank Gathers died — Abdenour wanted to know how fast the emergency unit could respond. When it arrived, Abdenour — standing outside the Palace — commended the unit for its speed.

■**MARCH 15:** With a 110-98 victory over San Antonio — their ninth straight and 22nd in 23 games — the Pistons overtake the Los Angeles Lakers for the NBA's best record.

■**MARCH 24:** Two days after Houston ended the Pistons' 12-game winning streak and 25-1 run, Dumars suffers a broken left hand in the fourth quarter of a 105-98 loss at San Antonio.

■**MARCH 26:** Swingman Ralph Lewis, a former Piston playing with Sioux Falls of the CBA, signs.

■**APRIL 10:** Dumars returns a week ahead of schedule, with six assists in a 108-98 victory at New York. The Pistons went 3-4 without him.

■**APRIL 16:** Indiana, coached by former Pistons assistant Dick Versace, beats Chicago,

Synchronized stretching played a main role in the Pistons' defensive scheme.

111-102, to clinch a playoff berth — and to clinch Detroit's third straight Central Division title. Assistant Brendan Suhr: "People said that we would be backing into it, and I just said, 'So?' "

■**APRIL 17:** The Lakers beat Seattle, 102-101, to clinch the NBA's best record.

PALACE MALICE

By Corky Meinecke and Drew Sharp

The Philadelphia 76ers didn't seem to feel any remorse about their role in a frightening brawl — one of the ugliest free-for-alls in NBA history — with the Pistons during the closing moments of their game April 19. It certainly didn't bother Charles Barkley, who was the life of the party in the Palace's visiting locker room after the Sixers' 107-97 victory clinched their first Atlantic Division title in seven years.

"I kick a--. I take names," said Barkley, who sent Pistons center Bill Laimbeer a note before the game. Several sports writers witnessed Barkley writing a two-word note, the second word of which was "you." He addressed it to Laimbeer, signed it "Charles," and had a ball boy run it over to the locker room.

Barkley ended a terrific night — 36 points, 15 rebounds — by rumbling with Laimbeer, who had shoved a ball into Rick Mahorn's face after Mahorn had dunked over Dennis Rodman with 14.8 seconds left in the game. Rodman fouled Mahorn, a former Piston, on the shot.

"They tried to start a fight with Rickey after the game was over," Barkley said. "I thought it

The Barkley-Laimbeer brawl produced a record $162,500 in fines. Bill Laimbeer and Charles Barkley were fined $20,000 and suspended one game (costing Laimbeer $8,000, Barkley $32,000). Scott Hastings was fined $10,000 and suspended one game ($8,000). Other fines: $50,000 for each team, $7,500 for Isiah Thomas and $500 for five Pistons and five Sixers reserves.

was a cheap shot." Barkley responded by unloading a roundhouse left to Laimbeer's cheek. Laimbeer absorbed another left to the face, then got in a couple of rights before he and Barkley were engulfed by a host of players, coaches and referees. "I can't believe he wanted to take my heavyweight crown," Barkley said. "I got in three or four punches, and I think I got the decision."

With Barkley on the floor during the scramble — which lasted several minutes — Scott Hastings left the Pistons' bench with his teammates, jumped on Barkley and landed what referee Jake O'Donnell called a "sucker-punch." As the officials tried to restore order, Barkley, bleeding from a cut on his left temple, grabbed a metal chair before he was restrained by an assistant coach. "I was just going to sit down," Barkley said later. The referees ejected Barkley, Laimbeer and Hastings; all tried to leave through the same tunnel, not far from the Sixers' bench. That's when an angry fan leaned over the railing and took a swing at Barkley, who climbed over the railing and spat in the man's face. That ignited another fight that brought players and coaches off the court and into the tunnel area.

The Barkley-Laimbeer bad blood started boiling March 2 at the Palace, after which Barkley vowed to "fight Laimbeer the first chance I get." In the April 19 rematch, Barkley and the Sixers gave the Pistons a little taste of Bad Boys-style

Jake O'Donnell and Palace security finally corralled Charles Barkley. When the Sixers returned home the next day, fans jammed the Philadelphia airport. "This is a great experience," Barkley said.

intimidation. When Laimbeer questioned a call, Barkley pretended to cry. When Laimbeer went to the bench, Barkley and Mahorn taunted him. Mahorn leveled Joe Dumars with an elbow to the head, and Dumars angrily grabbed Mahorn's jersey. A foul wasn't called on Mahorn, but rather on Rodman for grabbing Barkley.

Barkley, the league leader in technicals (29), ejections (five) and fines (more than $20,000), pulled no postgame punches, either. Told that Rod Thorn, the NBA's vice president of operations, would certainly fine and suspend him, Barkley said, "I make so much money, he can fine me as much as he wants." Told that Pistons coach Chuck Daly blamed Barkley for taunting Laimbeer, Barkley responded with a vulgarity, then said, "If he doesn't shut up, I'll go over there and rip that $300 suit off his back."

In addition to his first-half confrontation with Dumars, Mahorn took a punch in the head from Isiah Thomas in the second half. Thomas was ejected with 3:40 left. During the main event, Mahorn got face-to-face with James Edwards, perhaps his best friend the previous season.

"It's always disappointing when something like this happens," Mahorn said, "but you have to take care of yourself and not worry about what the other team does." As for Laimbeer's throwing the ball in his face, Mahorn said, "I guess it was his way of being tough." ∎

THE TEAM

John Salley was the Pistons' Crown Prince of Comedy, here getting chummy with Detroiter Carole Gist, who wore the crown of Miss USA. Meet the 1989-90 Pistons — from Worm to Buddha to ScottieWood.

CHUCK DALY

By Corky Meinecke and Charlie Vincent

Terry Daly can't count the games.

Surely, though, there have been thousands of them. In smelly, dimly lit gyms in little towns in Pennsylvania. In small college towns in Massachusetts. In the Carolinas and, later, much later, at the Spectrum in Philadelphia, Richfield Coliseum in Ohio and the Silverdome, then, finally, the Palace.

Thirty-four years of being married to Chuck Daly has meant 34 years of basketball. Of getting up in the morning and searching the sports pages to find out whether her husband's team won on the road. Of going off to sit in the stands to watch him work. Of screaming herself hoarse. Of savoring every victory and suffering with every loss. Of using the halftimes to compose herself, "to catch my breath like the players do."

On a Sunday morning in June she woke up with a strange sensation. "I got up at 7 o'clock with the dog," she said that afternoon, in the moments before the Pistons took the floor to play the Chicago Bulls in the seventh game of the Eastern Conference finals. "And all of a sudden it hit me: Oh, my gosh, this could be the last one. This could be the last game. It scared the devil out of me. I guess you don't realize some things until your back is to the wall. All of a sudden I realized I really do love basketball. It's not just a matter of providing for us."

Game 7 was not the last one — thanks to the vise-like defense that squeezed the Bulls so tightly they scored only 74 points, the fewest ever allowed by the Pistons in a playoff game. But most observers figured that the season's final series — against the Portland Trail Blazers for the NBA championship — would be the final games Chuck Daly ever coached. Probably he would quit. Go off to be a television analyst. Or a general manager. Remove himself from the locker room and from the daily stress of dealing with a dozen of the most talented, highest-paid and temperamental men in the United States.

It had been written he would do that. It had been said on radio and television, too. The first rumors started in December 1989. But Chuck Daly — 60 on July 20 and the NBA's oldest coach

— would never reveal his intentions during the season. And his wife could only say: "Everybody's speculating, but I honestly don't know where we'll be or what we'll be doing next year. And that's what was so scary to me Sunday. I knew it could be over, and I don't know where we're going to be next year. I honestly don't."

Chuck Daly is a private man. He does the commercials and his talk show and he will answer the questions about his team and his opponent's. But if you get into an area he would rather avoid, he will say something like, "Whatever," and change the subject or walk away.

Can you see yourself coming back next season, or would you rather be doing TV?

Whatever.

Is there something else you'd like to accomplish in coaching, or is money and security

your top priority?

Whatever.

How do you see your life changing after this basketball season is over?

Whatever.

The answer doesn't have to make sense, it has only to divert attention from the question.

What *does* Chuck Daly say?

He admitted that 1989-90 wasn't "the easiest of years," even though the Pistons posted the NBA's second-best record. Even before training camp opened, Daly had become "consumed by getting his team back to the finals," said Miami Heat partner Billy Cunningham, one of Daly's closest friends. When Cunningham coached Philadelphia, Daly was an assistant.

Daly's summer also was ruined by the unexpected departure of starting power forward

Chuck Daly, with help from assistant Brendan Malone and trainer Mike Abdenour, led the Pistons to their third straight Eastern Conference title.

Rick Mahorn, drafted by the expansion Minnesota Timberwolves two days after the four-game sweep of the Lakers. The Timberwolves made matters worse by trading Mahorn to the 76ers, who won three of four games from the Pistons and who Daly, on the eve of the playoffs, called "the favorite to win the Eastern Conference title."

Daly also had to deal with the return of center William Bedford, who spent the entire 1988-89 season in drug rehabilitation. Poor work habits and a cocky attitude made Bedford unpopular with his teammates. There were also doubts about small forward Mark Aguirre, whose excessive weight gain (to 250 pounds) coincided with a horrendous slump in the last two games of the 1989 finals — four points, 1-for-11 shooting.

The Pistons started slowly, but Daly's

decision to replace Aguirre with Dennis Rodman triggered a 25-1 run, the third-best streak in history. Aguirre initially accepted the demotion, but long stretches on the bench soured his attitude, and it strained the relationship between Daly and captain Isiah Thomas, Aguirre's childhood friend. Thomas, although reluctant to talk about Daly, said, "Every coach has pluses and minuses, but any time you can keep a team together this long and have it not explode in your face, you got to give the guy his due."

The Pistons finished 8-8 after the 25-1 streak, largely because of injuries to Thomas and to guard Joe Dumars, the team's leading scorers. During that stretch, Daly felt it necessary to explain his job situation to the team. "Basically," Dumars said at the time, "he got up and told us what was going on. I don't think it will bother this team. Maybe on another team it would. This team figures, 'Whatever happens, happens.' This team isn't going to huddle up and go, 'Oh, my gawd, this might be Chuck's last year.'"

After seven seasons Daly had won 369 of 574 games (.643). He had twice as many victories as any other Pistons coach. But his tenure had plenty of difficult times. General manager Jack McCloskey and Daly had a long history of contract squabbles. Daly worked without a contract for most of the 1986-87 season and throughout the finals of the 1987-88 season. He received an offer before the 1985-86 season to coach the 76ers, but the deal fell through after McCloskey demanded a No. 1 draft pick for letting Daly out of his contract.

Three months into the '85-86 season — after a stretch in which the Pistons lost 15 of 19 — the 76ers might have been able to pick up Daly for nothing. "My firing was imminent every night, from every direction, from upstairs to the media," said Daly, dismissed in Cleveland after losing 32 of 41 games during 1981-82. "And I had to answer the question every night. I was very aware of everybody involved, and what their thinking was." Daly paused and smiled. "Then the same team, with the same players and coaches, won 23 of 27 games."

Daly gained a measure of revenge by burying key McCloskey acquisitions at the end of the bench. For the most part, Daly all but ignored Bedford, McCloskey's pet project, and three free agents signed this season by McCloskey — David Greenwood, Gerald Henderson and Scott Hastings. "I wish," Greenwood said, "somebody would have told me he was like that."

Daly's '85-86 team foundered in the playoffs — losing to Atlanta in the first round — but the franchise has soared ever since. There are those who don't think Daly has received due credit —

from McCloskey and owner William Davidson, especially. He has come full circle, from offensive specialist to defensive strategist. His first team averaged 117.1 points, third in the league, and his 1989-90 team allowed only 98.3 points, best in the league. Opposing coaches run his plays and adopt his defensive philosophies. "Aw, I stole from everybody," Daly said. "If I didn't steal it from somebody in the league, I stole it from a coaching clinic I went to 25 years ago. Maybe I got it from Clair Bee or Frank McGuire or somebody. You steal it from everybody you can in this game. It's legal."

In 1989-90, only three players — Thomas, center Bill Laimbeer and guard Vinnie Johnson — and trainer Mike Abdenour remained from Daly's first team. "It's been seven very

Chuck Daly didn't always like what he saw. The players and assistant Brendan Suhr couldn't complain when Sports Illustrated picked the Pistons to repeat.

interesting years," Daly said. "It's been the highlight of my career, no question about that. I've never enjoyed coaching more. And no question it's been exciting."

And even though basketball has always been a family project, Daly has immersed himself so deeply in the sport that everything and everyone else are excluded. "It's a good thing I love basketball," Terry Daly said, "because I'm second to everything. I was able to accept a lot, and he always had a way of knowing when I'd had it. And he'd do something nice or say something that really meant a lot to me."

Daly's seven seasons were successful — and classy. He will be a difficult act to follow. ■

ISIAH THOMAS

By Michelle Kaufman

It happens every game, usually during the first few minutes of the second quarter. Point guard Isiah Thomas decides whether to take scoring into his hands or sneak out of the spotlight and let teammates take the shots.

"I have to play a different role every night at my position and try to balance the role as best as I can," he said. "You have to know when to back off. Some nights you read it right, sometimes you don't. It's a hard thing to do."

In two of the biggest back-to-back games, Thomas chose to take charge. In Game 7 against Chicago, he ended up with 21 points, 11 assists and eight rebounds. In Game 1 against Portland, he ended up with 33 points, six assists and seven rebounds. "I did what I had to do in order for us to win," Thomas said. "That's what I try to do every game. Sometimes it means scoring, sometimes it means holding back. Lately, I've been more of a feeder than a scorer because we have better offensive players than we had in the past."

Thomas, a nine-year veteran from Indiana, believes the start of the second quarter is the best time to map his game plan. "By that time, the game has developed some type of pattern," he said. "I know who's feeling good and who isn't, who's shooting well and who isn't. The stage is

Isiah Thomas, a nine-year veteran, played in the All-Star Game for the ninth time and started for the eighth time. He nearly won his third MVP, falling one vote shy of a good friend, Lakers guard Magic Johnson.

set. Definitely by the third quarter I know if I'm going to have to score a lot of points."

Once upon a time, he had no choice. His 20-plus points were counted on every game. If he scored a lot, the Pistons had a chance to win. If he didn't, they didn't. "It was a distraction," Thomas said. "You only think about numbers, and it's difficult to read the total game. I'd score 25 points, have 16 assists, and I couldn't tell you how we won the game. I like the mental part of the game and I missed that early in my career.'

But times changed. In 1990, he had Joe Dumars and Mark Aguirre and James Edwards by his side. He had Dennis Rodman and John Salley, who found joy in defense. And he had veterans Bill Laimbeer and Vinnie Johnson. Thomas' regular-season scoring average dropped from 22.9 points in his second season to 18.4 in 1989-90, but he didn't mind. He enjoyed his job more than ever.

"I have to think now and I like that," he said. "It's like a chess game every night. I get to read the whole game and get involved in the total package. My whole life I was the leading scorer. The star. 'Stop Isiah! Stop Isiah!' That's all people ever said. But I enjoy doing more than scoring. I like hurting teams with rebounding and passing and defense. Tell you the truth, I always considered myself a better defensive player than an offensive player."

There were times Thomas chose to lie low even though his gut told him to take over. He did it for the good of the team. "Sometimes I want to take charge and score a lot of points, but if I do that every night, the team gets accustomed to it," he said. "If you let other guys get involved, you're giving them a chance to get confident. Then, when it's time for the playoffs, we have eight or nine confident people instead of just two who can put the ball in the hole."

Entering the NBA Finals, six Pistons were averaging double figures in the playoffs. "That's unheard of in the NBA," Thomas said. "That's the reason it's so tough to beat us. We have 12 players committed to each other, even if it means giving up statistics. We're a very special team."

Just ask Dumars, his backcourt mate. "There are nights when he's the best I've seen at that position, at getting people involved," Dumars said. "He knows when a guy's hot and when he isn't." Though no longer the only Piston opponents must focus on, Thomas remained the central figure of the team. "He's still the leader, the captain, the nucleus of the team," Dumars said. "We've got 12 guys who can take care of themselves, so I wouldn't say we look to him for advice or anything. But there's no question the team still revolves around Isiah. He's the ignition. He's what makes the Pistons go." ∎

Although only 6-feet-1, Isiah Thomas never hesitated to drive on hulks such as Charles Barkley. Thomas and Joe Dumars formed one of the best guard tandems in NBA history. The best? Choose from Bob Cousy and Bill Sharman, Oscar Robertson and Jack Twyman, Walt Frazier and Earl Monroe, Jerry West and Gail Goodrich, Magic Johnson and Norm Nixon, Dave Bing and Jimmy Walker, and Maurice Cheeks and Andrew Toney.

JOE DUMARS

By Mitch Albom

One day, when the basketball is over, they can get down to being real friends. You can see them sitting at the beach, wearing shorts and polo shirts, trying to beat each other at checkers. Jordan will take the offensive. Dumars will counter with defense. One will grin. The other will nod. Respect. Admiration.

Friendship. One day.

Not now. Not on the court. Michael Jordan and Joe Dumars, Mr. All-World and Mr. All-World Stopper, put aside their fondness for each other and duel to the finish, move against move, every spin, every shot, every herk, every jerk. Take this, Joe. Swallow that, Mike. It is a backcourt

Joe Dumars increased his scoring average in each of his five seasons — from 9.4 to 17.8 points. He also worked hard on his free throws — going from 79.8 to 90 percent.

shadow dance that highlights each Pistons-Bulls showdown. Regular season or playoffs, we were watching basketball history. One day, they may talk about Dumars-Jordan in the same hushed tones as Chamberlain-Russell and Magic-Bird.

Wait a minute. Did we say friends?

Indeed. Dumars and Jordan. After five years of doing battle, they got to know each other at the All-Star Game in February 1990, when Jordan called down to Dumars' hotel room and said, "Why don't you and your wife come up and visit awhile?" They shared food. Talked for hours. Later Jordan would tell reporters, "Hanging with Joe was the highlight of my weekend."

Oh, don't worry. There would be no kissing at half-court. That's not their style. Both men shy away from public consumption. Besides, the public might have a hard time picturing Jordan, dripping with fame, exploding with flashy midair moves — a man Larry Bird once called "God in disguise" — chumming with the quiet Dumars.

But if you know the two men, you understand the relationship. Here was a perfect pairing of talent and humility, two guys who could dominate the sports pages, yet still mow the lawn at their parents' houses. They were born three months apart. They were both recently married. They began with only a basketball between them. It's just that, after all those nights battling each other, this nice thing called friendship began to stir.

"I guess it's mutual respect," Jordan said. "I'd always had tremendous respect for Joe. Then at the All-Star Game, I got to see him on the social side. He's a good guy, a quiet guy, not the type to search for stardom. I like that. We've built a friendship. Our wives get along great. I hope one day we can become best friends. But I'm sure he's not gonna let us get too close right now, and I understand that. You have to have complete concentration."

So while it is true, Jordan said, that he telephoned when Joe broke his hand in March, and Dumars telephoned when Michael was decked by the Bucks early in the playoffs, few words would be exchanged during the Eastern Conference finals. Who had time? Jordan was searching for a seam in a defense tracking him like a cruise missile. And Dumars was trying to bottle Hurricane Michael.

"There is nothing like it," said Dumars, shaking his head. "He is the biggest individual challenge you can have in this league."

No one has handled Jordan better than Dumars has. Detroit plays a tremendous team defense that lets as many as three players drop down to smother Jordan, block his path on the baseline, force his surrender of the basketball. But Dumars is the point man of this army. And for two straight years, Dumars won the war. With Jordan neutralized, the Pistons eliminated the Bulls in six games in 1989 and seven in 1990.

The Cyclone versus the Vacuum Cleaner.

What a wonderful rivalry! Two All-Stars. Two members of the all-defensive team. And you know what? You kind of hope they do wind up best friends. Then they can travel cross-country, stop at every high school, and show kids what you can grow into if you keep your mind straight and your talent exercised. Both Dumars and Jordan are textbook cases of The Graceful Superstar.

Not that they got there the same way. Jordan was a bright light from his freshman year in college, when he won the NCAA championship for North Carolina with a last-second shot. He was on the cover of Sports Illustrated before he could shave. He was a first-round draft pick — as a junior. He won Rookie of the Year, averaging 28 points, and served notice of his future stardom by setting new heights for dunks and reverse slams, prompting Nike to sign him and ride his rocket to incredible business. His contract with Nike is worth $12 million alone. Before his percentage.

Jordan has become a multinational corporation. Yet kids love him. So do their moms. "For all he's done," Dumars said, "you never see him shoot his mouth off, you know? He shows a lot of common sense. I guess that's why I like him."

Dumars can appreciate humility. His alma mater, McNeese State, was small and not far from his Louisiana home, and, unlike North Carolina, it never threatened anybody for a national championship. Joe was a quiet draft pick and arrived in Detroit playing defense and speaking only when it seemed appropriate. No Sports Illustrated covers. No huge endorsement deals. On his first trip to New York, Dumars stayed in the hotel, a bayou kid wondering why anyone would venture into that concrete jungle.

And yet, his talent, like Jordan's, was always there. And over time, it emerged. Partly because of his success against the likes of Jordan and Magic Johnson, Dumars began to attract attention for his shut-down abilities. He used to whisper to his teammates, "I can shoot if they let me." Eventually, they let him. Dumars became an enormous defensive and scoring threat, and certainly one of the four best guards in the NBA. He exudes the kind of leadership that is slow in coming, but unquestioned once it arrives. In June 1989 he was voted MVP of the playoffs. He had

reached the top. Quietly.

And it is a sort of quiet that he and Jordan share. Both men prefer simpler, more basic values and friendships that are strong even if unspoken. "I never tell Mike he's the best guy I ever played against," Dumars said, "and he never tells me I'm his toughest defender. There's no need. It's just understood."

Maybe it's in the blood. Both Dumars and Jordan come from large, close-knit families, where the men of the house did what they had to do without complaint. Joe Dumars II was a produce truck driver. James Jordan worked as a plant supervisor for General Electric. Hard work was the house rule for the fathers. It remains that way for the sons. So Dumars, despite his newfound wealth, goes back to Louisiana every summer and drives himself through daily three-hour practices in sweltering heat and humidity. And Jordan — who can't even count the interest

By hounding superstars such as Magic Johnson, Joe Dumars made the all-defensive first team for the second straight season. He also played in his first All-Star Game.

on his money — had a clause put in his contract allowing him to play whenever and wherever he wants in the off-season, no matter what the risk. That's how much he loves the sport.

Sounds like a hell of a rivalry, huh?

One day, when the basketball is over, they will sit around that beach and laugh at the memories. The friendship will wait. Good ones do. It says a lot that two NBA superstars, in a war for money and glory, can confess a fine and true affection for each other and a desire to see it grow. Mostly what it says is this: Sportsmanship is not dead. It's a pleasant thought. ■

DENNIS RODMAN

By Charlie Vincent

Usually, the moisture on Dennis Rodman's body is sweat.

Half his, half someone else's.

On this day, it was something else.

On this day, he could not help himself. On this day, he lost control, and the moisture on his body was the trail of tears that ran down his cheeks as he stood before the hot lights of the cameras at the Palace — on the eve of the Eastern Conference semifinals — and talked about what it meant to be voted defensive player of the year.

If there is one thing Rodman likes to do more than play defense, it is talk. And suddenly he could not talk. The words caught in his throat. The tears drained from his eyes. And he had to walk away from the microphone and around a corner where the cameras could not see him wipe away the salty joy of what he had accomplished.

People talk of basketball being a team game, all-for-one and one-for-all, pulling together and all of that. What Rodman does, though, is mostly one-on-one. Basketball lambada. Him on Charles Barkley. Him on James Worthy. And, in the Eastern semifinals, him on Patrick Ewing. And on Charles Oakley. And Gerald Wilkins. And Johnny Newman. "Against New York," Rodman said, with obvious relish, "I'm going to defend just about everybody. If they want me to go out there and defend the coach, I'll do that, too. To me, it's easy. It's just bump and grind, bump and grind, bump and grind. It's anticipating. I talk to myself all the time out there."

Rodman is never difficult to pick out on the floor. He is the one flying through the air. He is the one falling on the floor. He is the one with an arm-lock on an opponent. He never holds another player by the trunks, Rodman insists. But grabbing hold of an arm "just comes natural." He confesses to flopping, too. But his favorite dirty trick is the butt pat. "I think that's what they hate most," he said. "I don't know why, but when I pat 'em on the butt, they just hate it."

Some people play quiet, almost invisible basketball and contribute to their teams. Rodman plays the loudest, most visible basketball in the NBA, and May 7 his kamikaze style of defense was honored as the most effective in the league.

He thought he should have won the award a year ago, when Utah's Mark Eaton won it. Upset, Rodman called Eaton "just a shot blocker."

"I said some things that I shouldn't have said.

Dennis Rodman knew he had won the Defensive Player of the Year Award three days before the official announcement, but he cried anyway when Jack McCloskey told the press. Rodman received 49 votes, 14 more than Houston center Akeem Olajuwon.

That's not unusual," he said, able to laugh at his reputation for speaking first and thinking later. "To me, though, man-to-man, that's defense. It's a one-on-one thing. If I screw up, people will notice it."

So much is written and said about the athletes who have every chance, yet ruin their lives. More should be written about the Dennis Rodmans of sport. He had no chance, but saved his life anyway. He is an example of what sports can do for a man.

In Detroit, his story is no secret: lousy high school student; handyman at an auto repair shop; janitor at Dallas-Ft. Worth Airport who was taken in for questioning when he wound up with a pocketful of watches someone else had stolen; a dropout from the first college that took a chance on him before he became a three-time NAIA All-America at Southeastern Oklahoma State; and a high risk when, at age 25, the Pistons made him the 27th player drafted in 1986.

His is the kind of story that becomes a three-hour special on TV.

Rodman did not will himself to success. He worked himself to it. He knows what he is. And he knows how he is seen. And he has come to grips with both. "I may not be well-liked," he conceded,

As defensive player of the year, Dennis Rodman became the first Piston to win an NBA regular-season award since Dave Bing was rookie of the year in 1967. Rodman also made the all-defensive first team for the second straight season.

"but they say: 'He works hard.' People have called me a hot dog. Now people respect me as something." And you get the feeling that there is no way that he can find the words to tell you how important that is to him.

Dennis Rodman: Somebody.

Dennis Rodman: The best defensive player in the National Basketball Association.

Some might want to take some of the credit for that. Rodman even tries to share it. He says Adrian Dantley helped him. And Bill Laimbeer. And Vinnie Johnson. And Isiah Thomas. "A lot of times Isiah pumped me up," he said. "I needed motivation and he'd tell me, 'Go out there and kick some butt!' "

This day, though, was Rodman's, and his teammates would do nothing to detract from it. All his teammates left the Pistons' locker room while the press was huddled around Rodman. Someone wondered whether he knew what his award looked like. Is it a trophy? Or a plaque? Or a certificate? "I don't know what it looks like," he said. "But I've got it now. It's mine."

And where there had been tears of joy, there was a smile of pride. Of satisfaction. Of achievement. Dennis Rodman is the best darn defensive player in the NBA. ∎

JAMES EDWARDS

By Mitch Albom

He likes boats. He keeps one in a Detroit marina — complete with bathroom, shower, microwave and couch — and sometimes during the season he'll go down and sit in that boat, not going anywhere, just rocking on the water and taking it all in.

You can picture James Edwards that way, rocking gently, maybe a pipe slipped under that Fu Manchu mustache. Although he is an athlete in superb physical condition, there is something almost grandfatherly about him, something warm and sleepy-looking, a quality that has earned him the nickname "Buddha." Or maybe it's the company he keeps. After all, he was the oldest player on the team in 1989-90. Some of his teammates weren't even in high school when he turned pro. For a while, they might have called him "Grandpops."

Not anymore. "We're riding the Buddha Train right now," says John Salley, referring to the Pistons' success following Edwards' resurgence.

The Pistons were 7-5 and in second place when James Edwards replaced John Salley in the starting lineup.

"In practice, we say, 'Ride that Buddha Train tonight, baby! Buddha Train!' "

Well, you can't knock the ride. In November 1989, on a warm night in Sacramento, Edwards jogged out for the opening tap, alongside Isiah Thomas, Joe Dumars, Bill Laimbeer and Mark Aguirre. And Detroit has been almost unstoppable ever since. Funny, no? Here was an aging veteran who figured he was gone in the summer of '89. Had his bags packed. Then he became a star. Funny, but, for Edwards — who loves the water — this wasn't the first time the tide had changed.

"I was drafted by the Lakers in the third round of 1977, and nobody expected me to make the team," he said. "I remember Kareem (Abdul-Jabbar) told me not to get discouraged. Anyhow, I did make the team. Then, one night against Milwaukee, Kareem hits Kent Benson in the face, hurts his hand, and suddenly, I'm in the lineup. I'm playing a lot. As a rookie. Then Kareem comes back, and I get called into the office. Jerry West is in there. He says, 'We didn't want to do it, James.

But we traded you to Indiana. For Adrian Dantley.' Just like that. And I say, 'WHAT?' "

Thus began the education of a Buddha. He flew to Indiana that afternoon, landed in a snowstorm and played that night, alongside strangers. It would happen again in the years that followed in Cleveland, Phoenix and Detroit. "This is the NBA," he said to himself.

Not that it had been his lifelong dream. James Franklin Edwards, the only son of a Seattle engineer, was a reluctant athlete, a kid who liked to hang out by the water, a kid who shied away from aggression. But he was always so much taller than his schoolmates. And so he was nudged toward sports, until one day he said to himself, "I guess this is what I am supposed to do."

In 13 seasons, this is what pro basketball has given him: three trades, free agency, injury, wealth, two championship rings and a nasty drug controversy that left him believing "you can't trust anyone." No wonder he looks so . . . experienced. The drug thing was the worst. In 1987, Edwards and several Suns teammates were indicted on charges of trafficking cocaine and marijuana. It was an ugly, drawn-out affair. Eventually, Edwards was found guilty only of possession of marijuana and, after a year of counseling, his record was wiped clean. But the incident continued to haunt him. "I learned people will smile in your face," he said, "but be looking out only for themselves. I learned my lesson."

Detroit fans seem less interested in Edwards' past than in his present. His trademark fadeaway jumpers have been so consistent, the bench players yell, "FADE, BUDDHA, FADE!" Like a branding iron, he heats up quickly, often from the opening tap: bang, bang, bang, he's got six fast points. Then, when the opposing team doubles up on him, he swings the ball out to Thomas or Dumars for easy shots. He bangs his body and plays sticky defense. And the Palace crowd eats it up. "Buddha" has crept into its affection, not only because he is the type of hero who goes over well in Detroit — quiet, blue-collar — but because he did something few thought possible: He took the sting out of losing Rick Mahorn.

He talks of one day taking an easier road. Of putting the boat in the water near his native Seattle and "enjoying the peace and quiet." Third-round draft pick, three trades, one drug scandal, two championship rings and stardom. If you were to draw James Edwards' career, you might draw an upside-down Christmas tree, with all the presents coming at the top.

"Is it better to have success early or late in an NBA career?" he was asked.

He smiled and squinted.

"Better late," he said, "than never." ∎

BILL LAIMBEER

By Mitch Albom

They come at Bill Laimbeer like kids in a zoo. *Look at the beast. You think he bites?* This is Laimbeer's life, every day, in a restaurant, on the street. You can't hide when you're 6-feet-11. Even at home, he's sitting on his porch by the lake, and people approach in their boats and kill the engine and float past, staring, whispering, "That's him, there. Look."

Because he is 33 and a four-time All-Star, he ought to know better; he ought to fight the whole thing with a smile. And yet Laimbeer still hates this, the pointing, the questions, most of all the interviews, and so, usually, he reacts this way: He behaves like a jerk. He is good at it. Ask his teammates.

"I don't want anybody knowing any more about me than they have to," he admitted privately. "I don't want them to get to know the real me." And he makes sure of it. Laimbeer will slice and dice out-of-town reporters; they're in pieces when he's done with them. A month ago, inside Madison Square Garden, there was a triple execution. Three reporters in five minutes.

"Excuse me, Bill —" they began.

"What do *you* want? Who are you? Who do you *work* for?"

"Bill, I just wanted to ask a few questions—"

"About what? . . . That's a *stupid* question. . . . Who do you *work* for?"

"Bill, do you think the violence in the NBA—"

"I'm not talking about that. . . . Pick some other subject. . . . Who do you *work* for?"

He has a glare that could freeze a greyhound. He will sit in silence until you hear yourself sweating. He has created this image of Mr. Dirty Player, elbows and attitude. And besides that image, most reporters know nothing else about Laimbeer other than this: He is the guy who hears "SUCKS!" after his name in most NBA arenas. So they circle him like those kids in the zoo; some come to bludgeon him, others to poke and probe. There is this fascination in American sports journalism; we want to find a soft spot inside every monster. Does Laimbeer have one? The answer is twofold: 1) Yes, and 2) He'll be damned if he'll let you see it.

"You guys gonna stand there, or you gonna ask some questions?"

To watch Laimbeer in a group interview is to see a pose of intensity the way Rodin might have sculpted it. Eyes straight ahead, jaw clenched, hands locked together. Again, if he knows you, he will privately admit this is his defense against saying something foolish or explosive; he concentrates on every word as if he's passing a kidney stone. But that's if he knows you. And Laimbeer, a kid who grew up rich in Southern California, attended a high school on a cliff overlooking the Pacific Ocean — people could *honeymoon* in that high school — a kid who

temporarily flunked out of Notre Dame (lack of interest), never held a real job besides basketball and brags about how, when this career is over, he won't be staying in touch with too many of these people, isn't going to spend a lot of time getting to know you.

And here comes a question during the NBA Finals: "Bill, you guys shot 35 percent—"

"Thirty-six," he snapped. Eyes forward.

"Bill, Game 3 in Portland, can you win there?"

"We're only up to Game 2." Glare.

"Bill, have you ever thought about retiring?'

"Yeah."

There are times you want to smack Bill

Laimbeer — not because he's being a jerk to you, but because he's being one to himself. Away from the spotlight, Laimbeer actually can be intelligent, fairly humorous, and even has a kind streak. This is a guy with enough wit to whisper to Isiah Thomas after the captain hit those big shots in Game 1: "Isiah, you've always been my idol." Thomas cracked up. This is a guy who was quick to announce how much money he and Rick Mahorn would make off their Bad Boys poster the previous season. What he didn't announce was that he gave his entire share to charity, while Mahorn kept a lot of his.

Laimbeer is married to a sweet — and patient — woman named Chris. They lost a child once, a baby boy, born prematurely. Laimbeer will never bring it up. But he has talked about it. His friends talk about how he stayed at the hospital, so worried about his wife. He has turned red with embarrassment when his father called in a radio show and said, "Bill was always a good boy." He has agreed to a charity roast and was genuinely flattered that media people would sit on the dais with him. "Thanks a lot," he whispered, words you rarely hear from his mouth. You work in this town, you hang around Laimbeer long enough, you'll catch glimpses of this side he tries desperately to bury. It only makes you wonder why he wants to behave like a dork.

The center of opposing fans' bad intentions, Bill Laimbeer found a little love at the Palace.

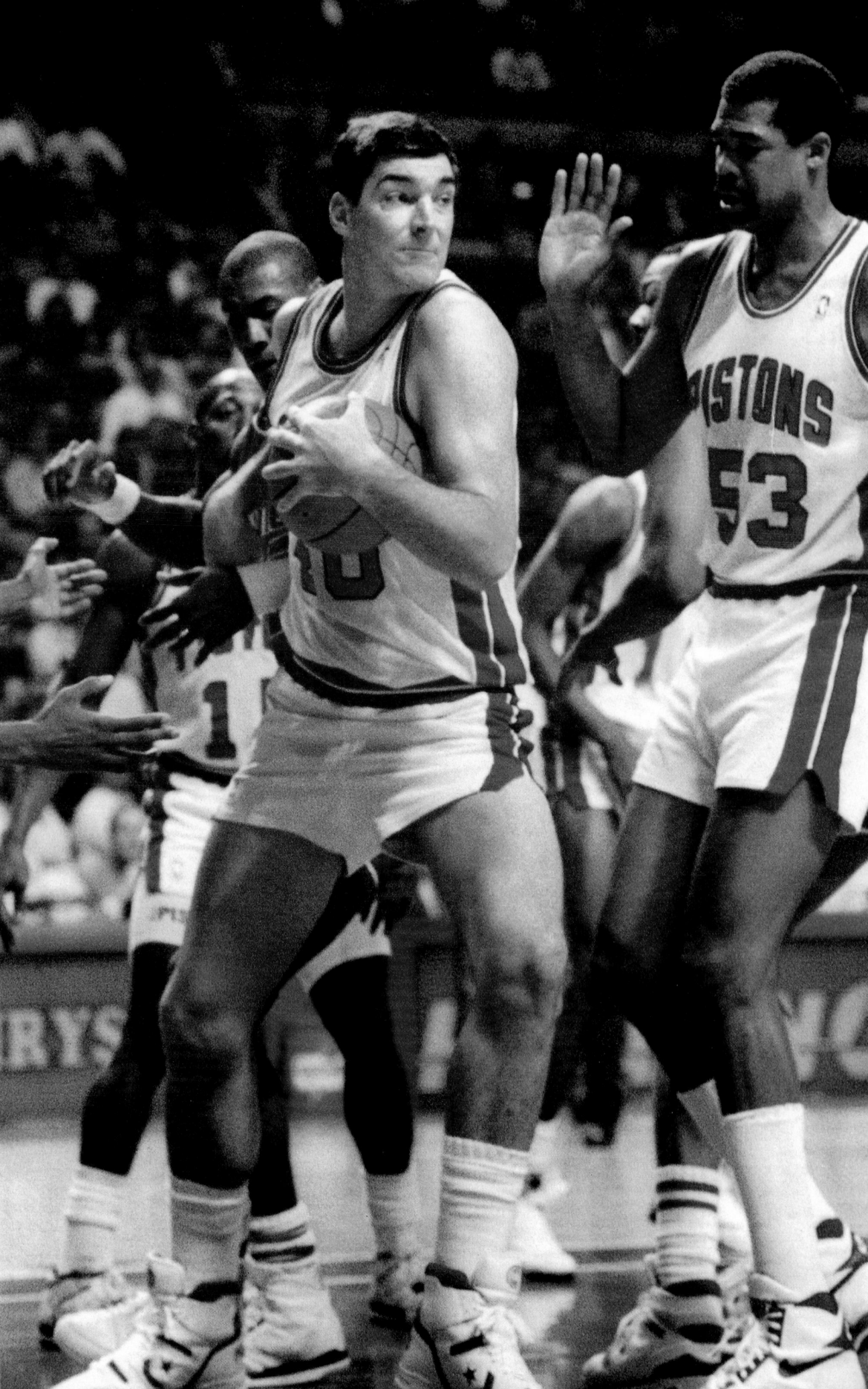

Has Laimbeer, after all these years, ever gotten comfortable with strangers asking him questions? "I never have," he said, suddenly candid. "You know, everything you do in this NBA life is watched by everybody. You live in front of 21,000 people a night. You can't go anywhere without someone pointing at you. You always hear somebody whispering, 'That's Bill Laimbeer. That's Bill Laimbeer.' That's why when people ask about my private side, it bothers me. It's like that's all I have left. That's why Isiah got so defensive when people were asking about his son last year. It's all you have that's yours. If they take that, they have everything. . . . You know, I'd like to go to a bar one night and get blind stinking drunk and be rowdy and carry on, but I can never do it as long as I'm a member of this team. I'd read about it in the newspapers the next day. I'm supposed to represent us in a certain way. I have to live up to the image."

You listen to that, you think, "Hey, maybe everyone is wrong about this guy." And then you think of the night in Atlanta, when they buzz-sawed a cardboard stand-up of Laimbeer during halftime. Zrrrrrp! Right across the middle.

But say this about Laimbeer: He takes his job at center seriously. Sometimes, work seems to be the only thing he believes in. He considered retiring before the season. Most people don't know this; he talked to Thomas about it. If you ask him about that conversation, he just says, "Isiah gave me a few good reasons why I shouldn't quit." You ask, "Like what?" and he says: "Money."

And once again, you're not getting the whole picture; it's doubtful any of us ever will. A lot of guys hate Bill Laimbeer — some of them wear basketball uniforms — and a lot of guys want to get his autograph. There's a guy (Scott Hastings) who came up with the T-shirts "Have You Hugged Bill Laimbeer Today?" But no reporter knows anyone who really knows him.

So he gets his wish, he goes on as a cartoon, the NBA villain, a role he laughs at, and why not? He helped create it. He feeds it. And, in turn, it cloaks him in a way that allows him to be nasty without disappointing anyone. Unfortunately, it doesn't always serve him well. He is smarter than you think, more charitable and more respectful than he lets on, but actions speak louder than words, and his actions are loud enough.

So ask him about rebounding. Ask him about defense. Ask him about another championship ring. If he's in a good mood, he won't chop your head off. He'll just leave you wondering, staring straight ahead. "How long after you quit before you go to that bar and get drunk and make a scene?" someone asked. He laughed, long and loud. "The *very next day!*" ∎

Bill Laimbeer, after leading the Pistons in rebounding for seven straight seasons, lost his title to Dennis Rodman, 9.65 a game to 9.63.

VINNIE JOHNSON

By Steve Kornacki

The Pistons have some of the most expressive faces in the NBA.

Bill Laimbeer has a scowl that says: "What's your problem, buddy? You've got nothing."

Dennis Rodman and Mark Aguirre are facial contortionists, twisting their cheeks and foreheads like dishrags. They scrunch up their faces after big plays and exclaim, "Yesssss!"

Isiah Thomas and John Salley are always smiling: Salley at his latest gag and Thomas at . . . well, what is he smiling about? Sometimes it seems as if he's the only one in on the joke.

James Edwards is majestic with his Fu Manchu, a contemplating Buddha of the paint.

Then you look down the bench at Vinnie Johnson and see. . . . C'mon, Vinnie, we're waiting. Show us something.

And he does, on the court. He shows his basketball stuff. It's rarely that his face tells you whether the shot went in.

Vinnie Johnson eclipsed the 10,000-point mark during the season. He played his best when a broken hand sidelined Joe Dumars, averaging 15.8 points in 11 straight starts.

Either way, there's defense to be played downcourt.

But in Game 5 of the Eastern Conference finals at the Palace, in which the Pistons beat Chicago, 97-83, for a 3-2 series lead, we found out what really turns V.J. on. It was assists. He had eight, and they weren't just another Microwave dish. They were special.

One pass was a study in the ball movement coach Chuck Daly deemed crucial in eliminating the Bulls. Johnson got Edwards the ball on the baseline but had it kicked back out to him. An open 12-footer was his, but he spotted Aguirre cruising alone to the hoop. Johnson put points in his hands. Then V.J. celebrated by whipping the ball backward between his legs a few times. Aguirre had been fouled and three points resulted. The next time down, Johnson set up Edwards for another three-point play. Johnson jumped for joy and waved his fist.

Danny Ainge nicknamed him Microwave because he heats up in a hurry. Turns out he can also set the table.

"I get respect as a player and shooter," Johnson said. "Most of the time, I get double-teamed by the Bulls. I've got to get it to the man who is open. That's when it's my job to create for other people."

As a fill-in for Thomas and Joe Dumars, Johnson, although 33, often made it hard to tell they were gone. He averaged double figures in scoring from 1983 to 1989. He averaged 9.8 in 1990. He sneaked into the team's career top 10 in points, steals and games played.

"I cannot say enough about the contribution Vinnie has given," Daly said. "He has been very aggressive taking the ball to the hole and passing."

And though the attention often goes elsewhere, V.J. is a solid fan favorite, much in the way Larry Herndon was for years with the Tigers. He's a professional's professional.

Winning is the only reward he wants.

"The games are different in the playoffs," Johnson said. "Every possession is important; every point means something. Everyone is focused."

He averaged 17.0 points in 1988-89 in the championship sweep of the Los Angeles Lakers. V.J. is a campfire waiting to blaze, but you could never tell it.

Don't read his face. Read the box score. ■

JOHN SALLEY

By Mitch Albom

With Rick Mahorn's exit, John Salley became the starting power forward, a job he lost to James Edwards in late November.

First, let's say that John Salley was funny in his debut as a stand-up comedian.

This was a pleasant surprise. There was reason to worry before the show in New York. A reporter found the 7-foot-tall Piston pacing nervously near the stage, and Salley looked at him and said: "Yo, you know any good jokes?" But, hey, maybe that's how Billy Crystal warms up. Of course, Billy doesn't often pepper the audience with giant people such as Dennis Rodman, David Greenwood, Scott Hastings and William Bedford. And they all sat together near the stage. When people yelled, "Down in front!" . . . they turned and said, "We *are!*"

This was an unusual night, April 9. For one thing, Spike Lee, the film director, was in the audience. His advice to Salley before the show was memorable: "Be funny, man." This was also an unusual night because proceeds from the show were going to benefit a 12-year-old boy from Brooklyn who had been severely burned by drug abusers after he refused to smoke crack cocaine. Salley had visited the boy at a hospital during the day. That was the hard part.

This was the easy part. Wasn't it? "I've always wanted to do this," Salley said before the show, as people filed in, and he greeted each one. "Comedians are my favorite entertainers. I've wanted to try this since I was 16 years old. But I'm nervous, man. Look at my leg. It's shaking. I've been worrying all day long about how I should open the show. They had this program on Showtime with all these young comedians, right? And I was thinking what if I just used one of their jokes? But then someone in the audience might yell out, 'Hey! I heard that joke on Showtime!' And I'd have to say, 'Yeah! So did I! That's why I'm using it!' "

He looked at the reporter. "What do you think?" The reporter told Salley not to worry, he could read the menu and it would probably come out funny. You see, Salley has had to do this his whole life. Stand up. Be entertaining. Critics say he does more of that than play basketball. But, hey, when you grow up that big and gangly, you

had better learn to make jokes first. Besides, by the time Salley was 10 he was going door-to-door in Brooklyn for the Jehovah's Witnesses, which matured him in a hurry.

"I'd knock on the door — this 6-foot-6-inch black kid, right, ringing your doorbell — and I'd say, 'Hello, my name is John Salley and I'd like to — ' WHUMP! Right in my face."

So he was prepared for a rough crowd. Remember, he plays for Chuck Daly. The other afternoon, Daly and Salley got into a shouting match that was captured on network TV. "Socks," Salley said. "We were arguing about . . . his socks. Yeah. That's it. I said you can't wear pink with green, Chuck. Get with it."

Back to the show. More people filed in. Salley seemed to know every one of them. Or he did by the time they sat down. ("Hello. How are you? You gonna laugh at my jokes tonight or what?") When Rodman walked past, he asked whether it was OK to use his video camera. "You're DENNIS RODMAN!" Salley bellowed. "You're an ALL-STAR! You can do ANYTHING YOU WANT!" "So it's OK, then?" Rodman asked.

Stricken with a sudden fear that no one would get his jokes, Salley rushed over to Spike Lee, who hadn't moved from his place at the center table. "Spike, man, what should I do?"

Spike said: "Do the funny thing."

Salley took the stage at the Stand-up NY Comedy Club to great applause. He waved and yelled, "WHAT'S UP?" And then he said. . . .

Well, can't print that.

After that he began to talk about his friends in the audience, especially this one who . . .

Um, can't print that.

He did introduce Scott Hastings. Can't print what he said. Oh, he did ask one guy with big ears to stand up, and Salley said, "I just wanted to show Dennis Rodman he wasn't the only one with ears like that." Everybody laughed, except Rodman, who was still trying to figure whether it was OK to use the camera.

And then Salley said . . .

Oops, can't print that either.

Anyhow, as the evening progressed, he got more comfortable and after a while was ad-libbing, which has always been his best sport. He announced that Magic Johnson was getting married, and some woman let out an "Awwwwwww," and Salley glanced at her and said, "Yeah, like you had a chance." Also, there was the time he identified a Detroit News sports writer in the crowd and said, "You gotta learn to stop writing in crayon, man."

In between Salley's bits, the real comics came up and did routines that included a lot of basketball humor. One said the New Jersey

John Salley worked well with his X Factor partner, Dennis Rodman. And he worked the crowd well during his debut at a comedy club.

Nets "are really making progress on that 25-year plan, huh?" He added that the sign in New Jersey where the team plays now reads: "INTERSTATE 95, Nets 91."

Then Salley did his closing monologue.

But you can't print any of it.

And so it's time for the four-star review: John Salley gets . . . three stars! Run and see it!

(By the way, it's not that the routine was dirty, it's just, well, think about Eddie Murphy or Robin Williams or Richard Pryor in concert. Think about printing some of that in a family publication. It's damn — uh — darn tough.)

For his part, Salley seemed relieved it was over. He said he might try again sometime, but not for a while. Too taxing. "It's like being at the free-throw line all by yourself, down two points with one second on the clock. I'd rather be laughing with my teammates."

After the show, the club owner, Cary Hoffman, was asked what he thought of the Piston as a comic. "He was great," Hoffman said. "He's a natural. I'd give him 20 minutes any night."

Hmm. That's about what he got from Daly. ∎

MARK AGUIRRE

By Corky Meinecke

The Pistons have asked a lot of small forward Mark Aguirre since acquiring him from the Dallas Mavericks midway through the 1988-89 season.

Change attitude. Lose weight. Play defense. Shoot less. Sit more.

No player wants to go from All-Star to seldom-star, but Aguirre has grudgingly accepted the plan. In January, he surrendered his starting position to defensive demon Dennis Rodman — a move that triggered the Pistons' 25-1 streak but doomed Aguirre to his worst statistical year in nine NBA seasons.

Aguirre, who turned 30 during the season, averaged 14.1 points — 4.5 points lower than 1988-89 and 10.7 points below his career average going into the season. He averaged 25.7 minutes and 11.5 shots — down from 33.8 and 20.4 in 1987-88, his last full season with the Mavericks.

"I'm trying to make it work for us," Aguirre said. "And I hope it's understood that I've been surrendering a lot of things."

In his wallet, especially. About a month before the Pistons sent Adrian Dantley to Dallas for Aguirre, Mavs owner Donald Carter orally agreed to double Aguirre's salary to $1.4 million. But a formal agreement was never drawn up, and the Pistons are bound only to a pact that will pay Aguirre $738,000 annually through 1996-97.

"I really don't like talking contract during the year," Aguirre said, "but I think something will be done after the season. Either way, something has to happen. As it is, I'm horribly underpaid. But Jack (McCloskey) knows basketball. If he feels he can use me, then he'll go ahead and do something. If not, then he might trade me. But it's a situation they have to look at next year."

When push comes to shove — as it usually does in the playoffs — Pistons coach Chuck Daly usually has eyes only for Rodman, who can smother everyone from 6-foot-6 Michael Jordan to 7-0 Patrick Ewing. Aguirre, at just 6-6, has trouble with just about every one of the league's starting small forwards. "I'll never be a great defensive player," Aguirre said, "but I'm better than I was when I first got here."

Daly might have given Aguirre a preview of things to come in a game against the Celtics on April 3. Aguirre never left the bench in the second half, mostly because Rodman had wrapped himself around Celtics star Larry Bird. The Pistons won by 11 points, holding Boston to just 82. "Well, Mark wasn't happy," Daly said, shrugging his shoulders. "And I knew Mark wasn't happy. But it's my job."

Aguirre insisted otherwise. "Hey, Worm was doing a great job against Bird," he said. "He was on a roll. You don't take him out in those situations. I was thinking about the win. Now, if I was thinking about my statistics and my contract, I would have been out of here last year."

Aguirre has been a puzzle to many coaches, but Daly claims to have "a pretty good feel for him." The coach sees a "multi-dimensional player who can do about anything he wants to do. He has amazing skills, and it's only a matter of how hard he wants to work on a given night."

Aguirre might be better off playing shooting guard, especially if Rodman remains healthy and

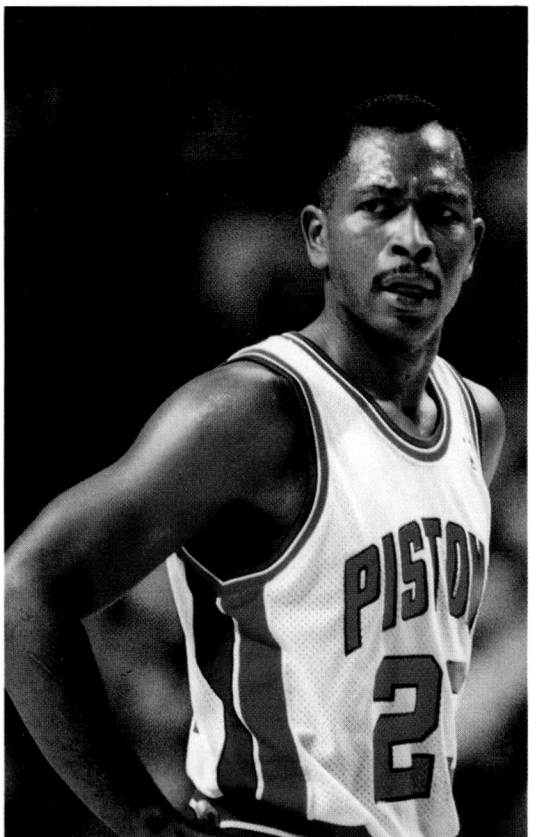

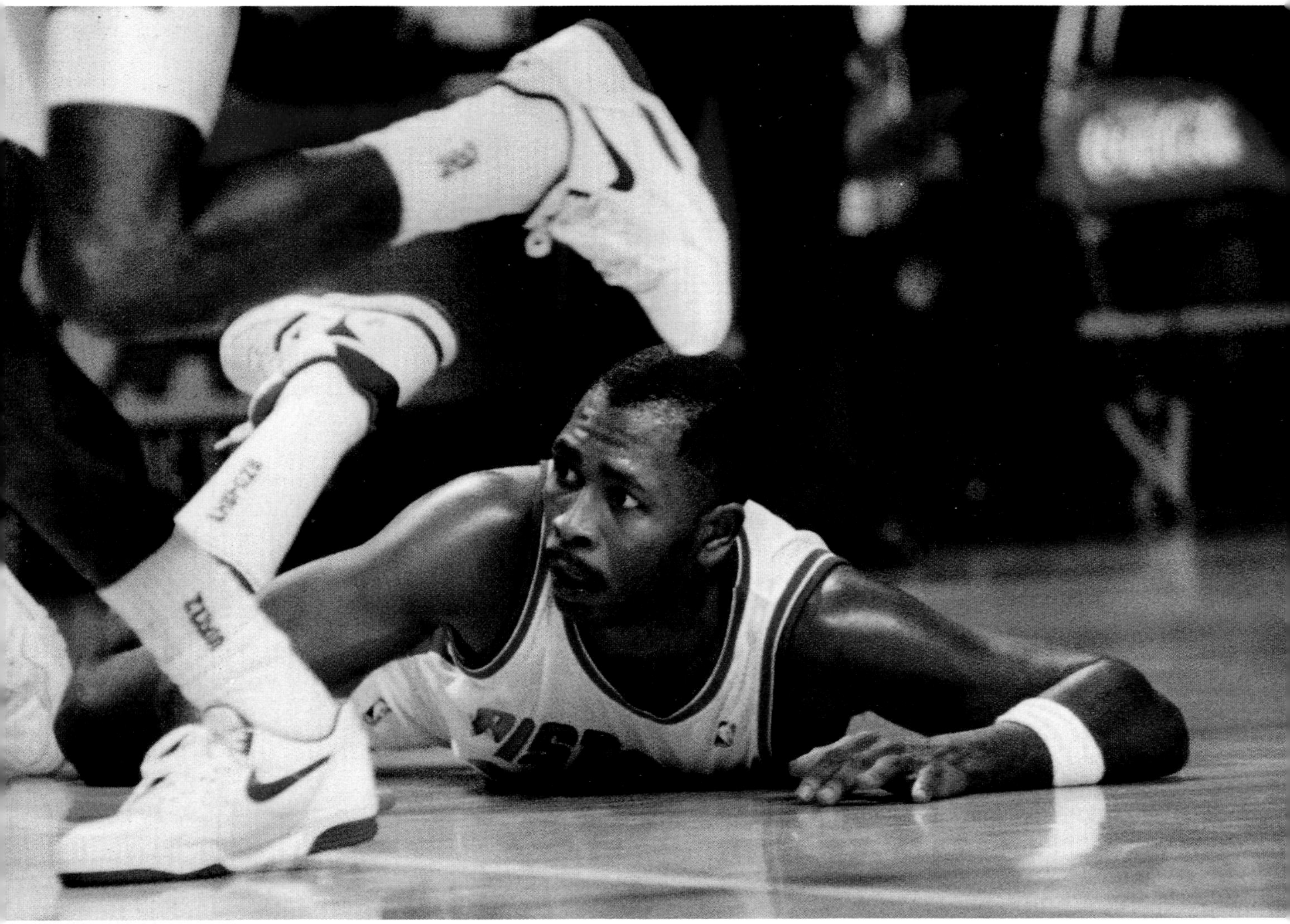

Although obtained in February 1989, Mark Aguirre didn't return to Dallas until March 1990. The Mavericks crowd booed him every time he stepped on the court or touched the ball. He scored 14 points — 12 in the first half.

productive. Daly experimented with Aguirre at that position, with mixed results. Aguirre possesses the required shooting and ball-handling skills, but Daly isn't sure how long Aguirre would be willing to chase the likes of Michael Jordan, Hersey Hawkins, Byron Scott and Ricky Pierce.

"He's capable, but his mentality would have to allow it," Daly said. "When he really wants to work at it, he can do it. I've seen him do it. He's very good at coming off screens and shooting jumpers, but he's reluctant to do that because he's never done it in his life. He'll have space to shoot, but then he'll take the ball into trouble."

Said Aguirre: "I can do it, but I'd probably mess it up for a while."

Aguirre isn't completely sure that the Pistons will come through with a new contract. He might mess that up, too. "But I would never regret my time here," he said. "I've had great fun. I've had the opportunity to play on a championship team, something not many people get to do. So far, it's been totally worth it."

So far. ■

GREENWOOD & HASTINGS

"Everything we do is insane. It keeps us sane."
— **Scott Hastings, philosopher**

By Mitch Albom

"So where's the popcorn?"

"Huh?"

"The popcorn. Don't you know the rules?"

"Yeah. Any fan sitting in that seat has to buy us popcorn. And beer."

"But . . . the game is going on!"

"We know that."

"Wait a minute. You guys eat during games?"

"Of course."

"When else?"

"Are you serious?"

"We're serious."

"And we're hungry. Get going."

Grab a sleeping bag. Fill the canteen. We are heading for The End Of The Bench. Which isn't exactly The End Of The World. It's worse. Even Columbus never looked for the End Of The Bench. If he did, this is what he would have found: Scott Hastings and David Greenwood, ordering popcorn. Not that they *eat* it. Oh, once, against the Knicks, Hastings, after countless nights of sitting, shoes tied, jacket on, and never playing, decided to sneak a handful. "And a minute later," he said, "when the kernels were still back in my wisdom teeth, and I'm trying to pick them out with my tongue, I hear Chuck Daly yell, 'SCOTT! SCOTT! GET BILL. GO GUARD PATRICK!' "

He panicked, right?

"No, I was happy to get in. And athletes are pretty superstitious. So we figure from now on, we should eat popcorn every game."

"Right," Greenwood said. "Popcorn. Good idea."

Hastings and Greenwood come out with the Pistons, night after night, race through lay-up lines . . . and sit. And sit. And sit. Occasionally, they get into the action, for a pass, or a free throw, or three minutes' worth of garbage time. "But basically," they said, "our job is to get stiff for two hours." They squirm; they scream at refs; they make up jokes; they check out the fan in the fourth row. They order popcorn.

This is the story of two men who have decided if you can't join 'em, joke 'em. Other stories have been written about the last guys on the bench. Usually, they carry quotes such as these: "I'm ready if the coach needs me. I don't mind waiting." Very nice. Very sweet. Complete bull. This is the real story. A world where boredom is the enemy, where humor is essential, where a "hello" from the head coach is a special occasion. A world where you rush to catch the bus because it might leave without you. Sitting? Watching? Who in his right mind wants to be one of the last two players off the NBA bench? It's grueling. It's frustrating. After careful study, Hastings and Greenwood have concluded there is only one way to avoid going nuts: Go nuts.

DAVE & SCOTTIE'S HOW TO AVOID BOREDOM, IDEA 87: TAKE A LAP

HASTINGS: We got the 20-second time-out down to a science.

GREENWOOD: *Yeah. As soon as it's called, we get up and try to circle the team while patting each of the guys on the butt —*

HASTINGS: *— and get back to our seats before the buzzer sounds.*

GREENWOOD: *One lap.*

HASTINGS: *One lap.*

GREENWOOD: *You can make it in just under 20 seconds.*

HASTINGS: *Of course, if you stop to say something, it takes longer.*

GREENWOOD: *Yeah. Usually you can only say, "Good job," and move on.*

Now, let's get something straight right from the start: Nothing Hastings and Greenwood do is meant to take away from the team. They root. They holler. They want to win just like the other guys. Why *else* would they go through all this sitting? But, yes, they sometimes scream

A Piston playing every second in all 82 games would have totaled 3,961 minutes. Scott Hastings played 166 minutes — roughly 4 percent of the time — and David Greenwood played 205 minutes — roughly 5 percent.

obscenities at the ref for a bad call, and then, the instant the ref turns their way, they spin their heads toward the stands and go, "Who said that?"

Maybe these two should go on the road. Live from Detroit, it's . . . ScottieWood! You ask how these guys can get away with all this stuff. Have you ever tried reaching the top of your profession — and then just watching? The distance between stardom and trivia is just a few yards on the NBA bench, but those few yards can feel like a chasm. It was into this breach that Greenwood and Hastings tumbled in 1989-90. Unlike many 11th and 12th men, they were not rookies, not kids all starry-eyed and "happy to be here." No. They were veterans who knew better. They grew friendly. They grew close. Now they are Martin and Lewis.

DAVE AND SCOTTIE DISCUSS FEAR

GREENWOOD: *Unlike some others, we never root for the starters to get in foul trouble.*

HASTINGS: *Yeah, because our biggest fear is that the starters will all foul out and they'll actually use Vinnie Johnson at power forward before they use us.*

GREENWOOD: *Who needs that kind of embarrassment?*

HASTINGS: *Really.*

We might have seen this coming with Hastings. Wasn't he the Atlanta Hawk who once slapped high-fives with owner Ted Turner after sinking a three-pointer? Wasn't he the guy who wrote a column for the Miami Herald last year as a player for the expansion Heat? Didn't he once suggest the Heat's losing streak could be solved with three easy steps: 1) Keep working hard. 2) Pick a fight with every opponent averaging more than 20 points. 3) Trade for Magic Johnson, Michael Jordan and Karl Malone. Hastings, 6-feet-10, is a Huck Finn face stuck on a giant scarecrow body. If he can't make you laugh, you're medically dead. They call guys like Hastings "free spirits" — usually right before they call them "free agents." That's what he was in July 1989. After stints with New York, Atlanta and Miami, he signed with the Pistons.

Greenwood came a few months later. He, too, was a free agent and was coveted by several teams. But, at 32, a new team wasn't enough. He wanted a ring. Coming out of college he was a star, the second player taken in the 1979 draft. Unfortunately, the first was Magic Johnson, who went to Greenwood's desired team, the Lakers. Greenwood went to Chicago. He suffered there until the arrival of a kid named Michael Jordan — then the Bulls traded Greenwood to San Antonio. He suffered there waiting for a kid named David Robinson — then the Spurs traded him to Denver. "I figured Detroit could use me, since they had just lost Rick Mahorn," he said. So he signed in October. A one-year deal. A slow training camp hampered him. Then the improved play of James Edwards, John Salley and Dennis Rodman left little room for his 6-foot-10 presence. Suddenly, the former hero of UCLA found himself in the last seat on the Detroit bench. "I said to Scottie, 'I'm not used to this, man. If you ever look over at me and see me losing it, you gotta help me, OK?' "

Scottie nodded. He knew just what to do.

DAVE AND SCOTTIE'S HOW TO FIGHT BOREDOM, IDEA 128: CHEW A TOWEL

GREENWOOD: Scottie has this thing during the game where he just chews the end of a towel until he can pull a string out between his teeth.

HASTINGS: I used to leave it hanging there just to hear people yell, "Hey, you got a string hanging from your mouth!"

GREENWOOD: Then one day he started blowing them onto people.

HASTINGS: They're just little threads. Sometimes James Edwards will come over, and he'll be all sweaty. I'll blow one at him.

GREENWOOD: And it sticks.

HASTINGS: Yeah. It's pretty cool.

Everyone thinks the same thing. Goodness. All that money and so little work and these fellows are having . . . fun? Well, before you condemn it, remember that these fellows, despite their spots on the bench, are still better than 97 percent of the basketball players on this planet. That's the crazy thing about the NBA. You take a guy who was king of his high school, prince of his college, and, suddenly, in the pros, he's the mop-up man. "I don't care if you're Mr. Optimist of the world," Hastings said in a rare serious moment. "Nobody can sit there and watch his job being done by someone else and feel like he's contributing."

"I never used to think about bench guys when I was a starter," Greenwood said. "I've gained new respect. It's one of the hardest things to do. And garbage time doesn't cut it. I'll be honest with you. Going into a game with 30 seconds left and a 35-point lead — that's not playing basketball. It's almost like an insult. That's like saying the guy ahead of you can't last another 30 seconds, so *you* get in there. Garbage time is a lose-lose situation. If you play well, they say, 'Aw, it was just against the other team's scrubs.' If you make a mistake, they say, 'See? That's why we can't play him.' "

Hastings agreed. "I went into a game with 12.8 seconds left and came out with 11.6 left."

"Amazing," Greenwood said.

"Yeah. I got what we call a trillion."

A trillion? "Yeah. That's when the box score reads: '1 minute played, followed by a row of

0-0 0-0 0-0 0 0 0.' I got lots of those."

DAVE AND SCOTTIE ANSWER THE QUESTION: WHO ARE WE?

GREENWOOD: Honest now, Scottie, when was the last time a coach came up and said, "Hey, how you doing? How's your wife and kids?"

HASTINGS: Never!

GREENWOOD: See? We do not exist.

HASTINGS: Right. We are like the twins that the family hides in the basement.

GREENWOOD: We are like professional blackboards. There's nothing there.

HASTINGS: We are like the insurance policy that you get when you're first married—

GREENWOOD: — and then you stick it in the attic —

HASTINGS: — and 40 years later you dust it off and say, "HEY, HONEY, LOOK WHAT I FOUND! IT'S DAVE AND SCOTT!"

Often, when a Piston is having a bad stretch, he will come to the bench and get an earful from Daly. Then he'll wander to Hastings and Greenwood, who he knows have been watching. "James, you drove the baseline the last five times.

Go to the middle next time," they'll whisper. "Salley, stop thinking so much and just go up with it." Often, the advice is good. And when the guy goes out and sinks a basket, he turns to Greenwood and Hastings and points and smiles.

Sometimes, however, even the jokes can be painful. Once, Hastings and Greenwood were giving referee Darell Garretson a tongue-lashing. Finally, Garretson turned and said, "Hey, you getting in the game tonight, Greenwood?" Ouch.

It's not easy, this life of understudy. It's dull and it's agonizing and you always feel you should be doing more — especially when you've put in your time in the league. "Guys on the team ask us why we're cheering so much," Greenwood said. "But I say, 'Wait a minute. I didn't sit on this bench all year so we can *lose* the championship. Are you kidding? I WANT A RING!' " He turned to Hastings. "And he wants a Porsche 928."

If you can't join 'em, joke 'em. Live from Detroit, it's ScottieWood! By the way, should you go to a Pistons game and sit alongside these two and they turn and ask you for the popcorn, remember this: They're only kidding.

Now, about the beer. . . . ∎

GERALD HENDERSON

By Drew Sharp

Deciding whose offer to accept was easy for Gerald Henderson. He wanted to go to the team that provided the best chance for his third NBA championship ring.

Henderson joined the Pistons Dec. 6 after signing a one-year contract. He replaced Stan Kimbrough, a rookie guard from Xavier (Ohio) who rarely played and was waived.

"I've already won two rings when I was with the Celtics," said Henderson, who selected the Pistons over two other teams he did not identify.

"I'd love to get No. 3, and these are the defending champs. I think this will provide my best situation. I'm very excited about being here."

Henderson was a bargain. Milwaukee, which waived him, had to pay all but the NBA-minimum $110,000 of Henderson's guaranteed contract. The Pistons picked up the rest — only a prorated $88,771.

Henderson, acquired while guard Vinnie

Gerald Henderson won NBA titles with Boston in 1981 — when he averaged 7.8 points — and in 1984, when he averaged 11.6.

Johnson was mired in a terrible slump, gave coach Chuck Daly another backcourt option. Henderson also provided insurance — much the way guard John Long did late in the 1989 season after he was claimed off waivers.

For Henderson, at the time 33, the Pistons were the sixth team in an 11-year career. He was cut by Milwaukee Nov. 27 after guard Paul Pressey returned from the injured list. Henderson was picked by the San Antonio Spurs in the third round of the 1978 draft, from Virginia Commonwealth. His career average entering the season was 9.7 points; in 11 games with the Bucks, he averaged 2.5. He would average 2.3 in 46 with the Pistons.

"I consider myself the type of guard who's comfortable at either spot," Henderson said. "However they want me to contribute is fine with me. When you've been a reserve for most of your career, you learn that you have to always be prepared to come in at any time."

That's the veteran attitude the Pistons were looking for. ∎

WILLIAM BEDFORD

By Drew Sharp

William Bedford shook his head and sighed as he walked to the Adult Substance Abuse Program clinic in Van Nuys, Calif. But any apprehension disappeared as he walked inside and was greeted with hugs from two of his counselors.

"Look at you. Man, you look great," said Dr. Rex Fine, ASAP's program director. "Didn't recognize you with the smile on your face."

The staff was pleased to see one of its successes, as Bedford continues to maneuver the high wire that separates a recovering substance abuser from a relapse. "How are you doing, William?" asked counselor Tony LaFargue.

"I made it to today," Bedford said, smiling.

This was Bedford's first visit — on Dec. 1 — to the Adult Substance Abuse Program treatment center since his return to the Pistons after an 18-month suspension. The visit was an informal portion of Bedford's aftercare treatment; the staff always wants to see former patients when they are in Los Angeles. Bedford and Fine laughed, but during Bedford's stay at the center there had been few funny moments. There had been angry words, a few thrown chairs in the tug-of-war to make Bedford accept his illness. It took nearly a year. The moment came Jan. 13, 1989, the last time Bedford used cocaine. Bedford returned to the clinic with his second strike and was one offense away from a two-year NBA banishment. "I've been clean ever since," Bedford said. "I've got the date down. At that point, I realized my life was disintegrating right before my eyes."

Bedford's candidness pleased Fine, who not so long ago knew a more sullen, reclusive Bedford. "He looks as though his soul has been cleansed," Fine said. "I could tell as soon as I looked in his eyes. They sparkled. He looks as though the pressure of the world has been lifted from his shoulders." Bedford nodded in agreement.

"William was angry and stubborn," Fine said, "but so was I. I wasn't giving up on him." Bedford's gratitude was evident as he listened to Fine and LaFargue reminisce and laugh. "I don't think I could ever just walk away five years from now and think I could do without them," Bedford said. "I love these guys. They saved my life." ■

Midway through the season, William Bedford received a three-year contract. A professional for four seasons, he had played only 130 games.

MIKE ABDENOUR

By Corky Meinecke

Joe Dumars, a rookie guard from McNeese State, watched in awe from his seat on the bench as Pistons trainer Mike Abdenour scurried here and there, picking up towels, scribbling on clipboards and screaming at everyone — the Pistons, the opponents, the referees. "I turned to somebody and said, 'Boy, he's really into the game tonight,'" Dumars said, recalling his first NBA game. "Little did I know — five years later, he's the same way. Every game."

"My first impression of Mike?" captain Isiah Thomas said. "Well, my first impression of Mike was that he was a very nice person, but that he had this problem — hyper, real hyper."

A Tasmanian Devil with tape.

That's Mike Abdenour.

"Many trainers try to be unemotional," assistant Brendan Suhr said. "You'll see them on TV, sitting there with their legs crossed during a one-point game. Mike can't do that."

Abdenour, at 37, has been in the Pistons' corner for 15 years — longer than anybody in the organization with the exception of team physician Dr. Ben Paolucci, scout Will Robinson and equipment manager Jerry Dziedzic. He was hired part-time in the fall of 1974, when the Pistons played at Cobo Arena. The coach was Ray Scott, the stars were Dave Bing and Bob Lanier, and the pay was $15 a game. Today, Abdenour's training room at the Palace is "bigger than the press room, locker room, training room and storage area combined at Cobo," he said. Should the players again vote him a playoff share, Abdenour's earnings will approach six figures. "He's still underpaid," Suhr said.

Abdenour is everything to everyone — morning, noon and night, during the regular season, in the playoffs and throughout the summer. Need 18 hotel rooms at a moment's notice? Call Mike. Need 50 pieces of baggage delivered from the hotel to the arena? Call Mike. Need reservations at the best restaurant in town? Call Mike. Need directions to the best restaurant in town? Call Mike. Need a shoulder to cry on? Call Mike. Need anything at all? Call Mike. "It's not just taping ankles, that's for sure," said

Abdenour, a Wayne State graduate whose younger brother Tom is the Golden State trainer.

It's remaining neutral when a problem arises between coach and player. It's making everyone's life easier but your own. It's having a soft heart and a thick skin. It's getting blamed for things over which nobody has control.

"I don't remember where we were going," Thomas said, "but we had a layover and the flight was delayed. Chuck (Daly) turns around and starts yelling at Mike for the flight being delayed. I'm sitting there thinking, 'What does Mike have to do with United Airlines?' "

Daly smiled and said, "Mike is, uh . . . " Then he paused and smiled again. "He's kind of a Damon Runyon character in the league, both in and out of uniform. In a lot of ways, he's overqualified for the job. He knows enough to coach the team. He knows enough to fly the plane. And he knows enough to be the doctor. When he gets involved, he sometimes gets so involved that it can drive you crazy."

Some trainers calmly occupy the end of the bench; Abdenour prefers the seat next to assistant Brendan Malone, one space from Daly. During time-outs, he stands, back to the huddle, scanning the opposing bench for lineup changes, and the immediate area for nosy TV cameramen. His voice is one that can be heard above all others, no matter how noisy the arena. And he never gives it a rest. He helps the coaches coach, the players play and the officials officiate. Three times he has been whistled for technical fouls, an unofficial record for trainers. "Jack (McCloskey) has told me, 'Don't get the fourth,' " Abdenour said. When Daly decided to take the Pistons to Miami a day earlier than planned, Abdenour called a hotel representative 11 times in two days, trying to get rooms. Each time the answer was no, "but I don't take no for an answer," he said, smiling. "That's what the boss wanted, and I'm here to take care of the boss. That's my job. And I'll do whatever I can to make everybody else's job easier. My philosophy is: I'll do whatever it takes to win."

Abdenour is best at getting injured players back into the lineup. In 1988-89, Thomas played through a broken hand and Bill Laimbeer an ankle fracture. "The peer pressure on this team," Abdenour said, "just doesn't allow anyone to take a night off. Bill chases guys out of my training room. That makes my job a whole lot easier."

Abdenour has visions of someday making the transition from the locker room to the front office, but "I wouldn't know how to go about it. Do I want to die on this job? I'm not really sure."

Laimbeer is: "He's a Piston. Always has been, always will be." ∎

With Mark Aguirre dazed and confused after colliding with James Worthy, Mike Abdenour came to the rescue.

THE MODEL FRANCHISE

By Corky Meinecke

None of it seemed to make sense.

Not abandoning the Silverdome, where a then-NBA-record 1,066,505 saw the Pistons play during the 1987-88 regular season; not building the Palace, a privately financed arena dependent on the marketability of 180 luxury suites; and not purchasing private jetliner Roundball I, which has proven to be twice as expensive as commercial air travel. "Fortunately," said Tom Wilson, the Pistons' chief executive officer, "we have an owner who is a bit of a visionary. He sees things five years in the future and beyond."

Lending a deaf ear to conventional wisdom, Pistons owner William Davidson turned his back on the Silverdome, then stuck out his neck on the Palace and Roundball I. Those moves, combined with innovative marketing and broadcasting campaigns, have put the Pistons in position to dominate what could be the NBA's soaring '90s.

On and off the court, the Pistons are trendsetters. League owners make the Palace their first stop before proceeding with plans for new arenas; general managers take note of Jack McCloskey's drafting and free-agent signings; coaches copy Chuck Daly's offensive sets and defensive theories; marketing and television directors listen closely when Wilson and his staff share ideas.

"I think they've done an unbelievable job," said Greg Jamison, vice president of business operations for the Indiana Pacers. "I've been in the league since 1980, and I remember how they were viewed then. They've done some wonderful things, culminated in the building of a beautiful arena."

"We're the showcase of the NBA right now," said Ron Campbell, the Pistons' director of finance.

And the Pistons are the biggest cat in a state that used to be dominated by Tigers and Lions. "There's no question we're envious of their success and their stature," said Chuck Schmidt, the Lions' executive vice president and chief executive officer. Said Campbell: "When we go to league meetings, you always hear, 'Well, this is how the Pistons do it.' It's hard to be humble."

Tom Wilson and Jack McCloskey are men of letters — CEO for Wilson, GM for McCloskey.

And hard not to gloat.

When the Pistons announced plans to leave the Silverdome, "the only thing everybody agreed on was that the area didn't need another arena, and that it wouldn't make it," Wilson said. And when the Pistons announced that the $70 million arena would feature 180 luxury suites, "Well, that was just ludicrous," Wilson said. But the Pistons found a renter for every suite, including the 16 most expensive ones — $120,000 annually, 16 rows from the floor. The Palace guaranteed 100 events, delivered 167. Suite revenues, about $12.1 million, are paying off the Palace mortgage. "We built it backwards," Wilson said. "It became a thing where the suites made the building possible."

Nothing was too good for the Palace, regardless of cost. It got the finest scoreboard, the best sound system. Cushioned, cloth seats instead of vinyl. A $2-million television studio. A spacious locker room, with saunas, whirlpools and the latest in weight-training and exercise equipment. Plush offices, meeting rooms, a restaurant and lounge. "There's a standard for arenas, and then there's our standard," Wilson said. "The organization is like the team in that there's an accepted level of performance, and you don't slack off or screw off. If you have an opportunity to see a game at the Palace, it should be a big night."

Campbell declined to open the books, but the Pistons' profits are thought to have exceeded $14 million for the 1988-89 season. Campbell would say only that the Pistons are "very comparable" to the Boston Celtics, a publicly owned club that made $12.2 million. Campbell stressed that the Pistons and the Palace were "two different entities, run two different ways." All money from suites, concessions and the TV studio go to the Palace. Campbell said the Pistons pay rent to the Palace — "about the same amount as we did at the Silverdome," about $1 million. Of course, the distinction may be moot; the Palace and Pistons are owned by the same partnership, headed by Davidson.

The regular season ended with the Pistons' 91st straight sellout (21,454). At an average ticket price of about $25, it translated into a gate of roughly $500,000 — not including suite revenues. Revenue from local broadcasts, carried on WKBD-TV (Channel 50 in Detroit) and PASS cable, was about $8 million. From CBS and TNT cable, the club received $2.8 million. Local radio, WWJ-AM, brought in another $1.4 million. Also producing revenue were four Great Stuff stores, which sell Pistons and other sports merchandise. The stores have been a huge success. Buoyed by a championship season — and Bad Boys hysteria — sales of Pistons merchandise exceeded $30 million nationally in 1989.

Coaches and players rake in the money, too. All are in great demand for clinics, appearances and autograph sessions. Daly has a TV show, and several players have radio shows. Daly, Isiah Thomas and John Salley sell cars on TV. Joe Dumars signed a lucrative deal to be spokesman for the Michigan Lottery. Bill Laimbeer hawks boats; Vinnie Johnson, pizzas.

Joe and Jill Fan haven't been as fortunate. Moving from the Silverdome to the Palace required 186,891 fewer fans to pay more than twice as much — from about $10 million to $21.5 million in ticket sales — for 41 regular-season games in 1988-89.

Roundball I is the team's biggest expense. Many NBA teams charter jets from time to time, but none has made the Pistons' total commitment "because it makes no sense financially

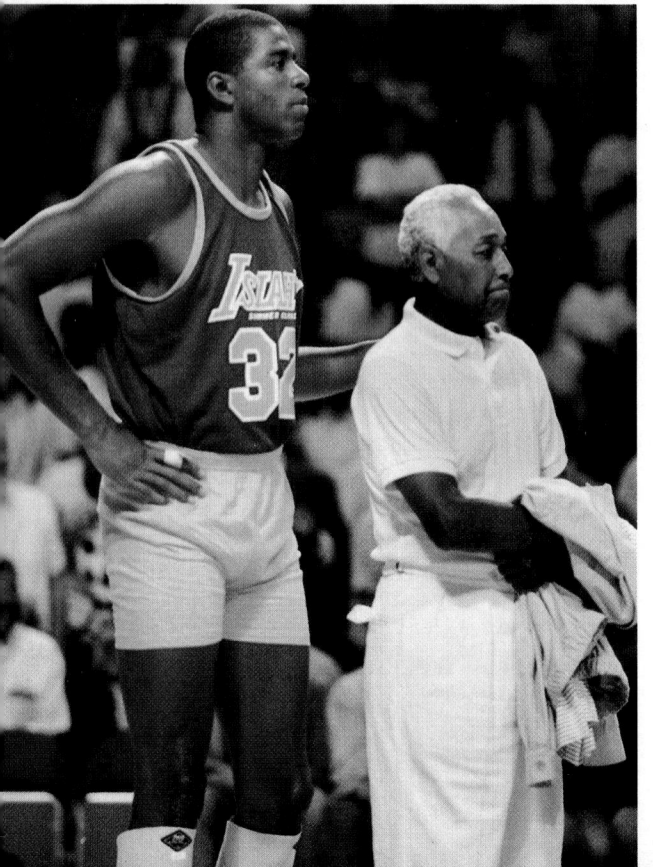

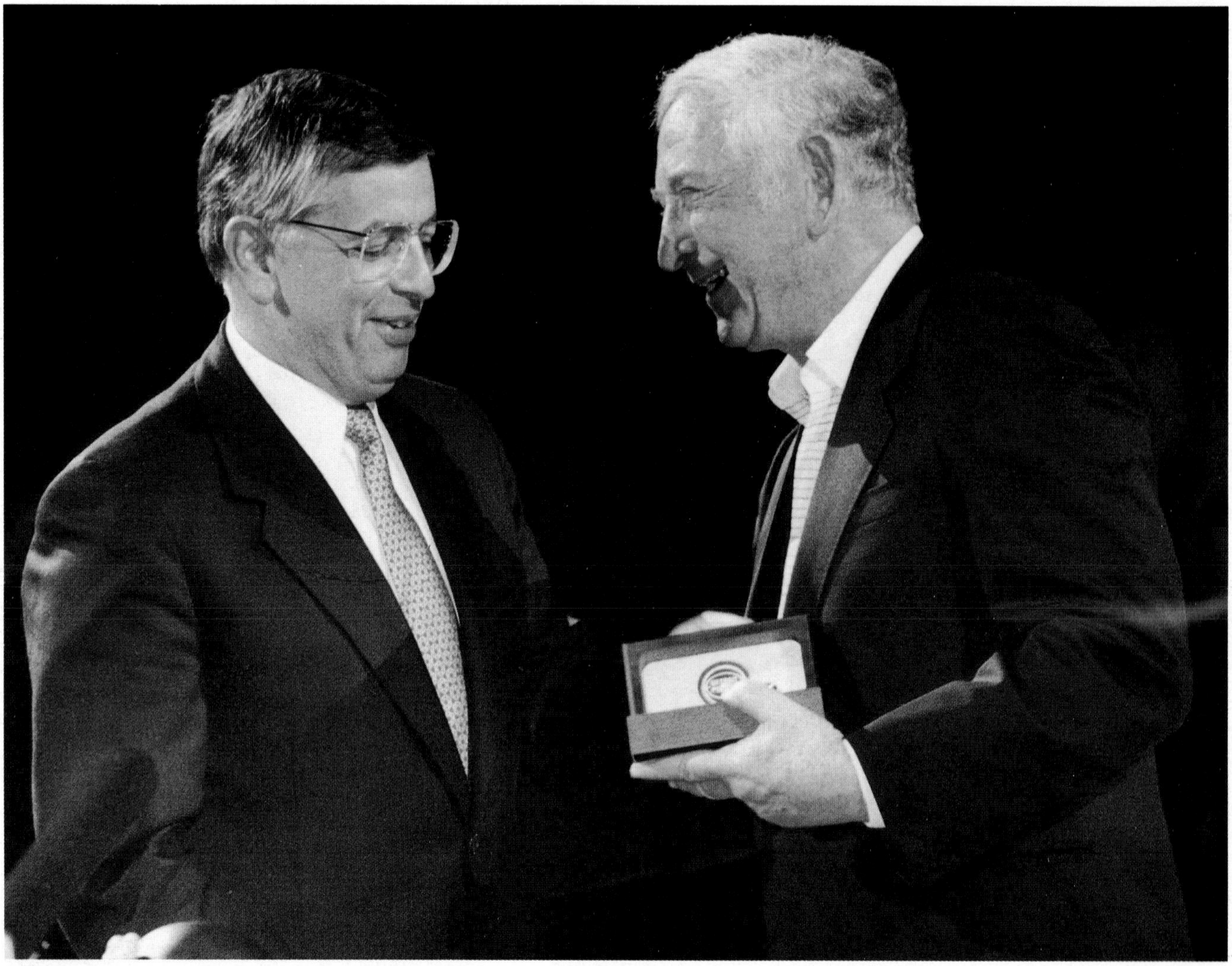

Commissioner David Stern had a ring for William Davidson. Will Robinson, an administrative assistant who specializes in scouting, had plenty of magic moments as a prep and college coach. He got to coach Magic Johnson in Isiah Thomas' Palace all-star affair.

whatsoever," Wilson said.

The estimated cost of the plane was $1.2 million, "but by the time we got going," Campbell said, "it was double that." And after further improvements last year, the price had jumped to $4.5 million. That doesn't include yearly operating expenses, which exceed commercial travel by $500,000 to $1 million.

"Well," Davidson said, "you have to figure in the differences, and if you're getting value for those differences."

In 1986-87 and 1987-88, the two seasons before Roundball I, the Pistons were a .487 road team (40-42). With Roundball I the last two seasons, the Pistons are 50-25 (.666) away from the Palace. Not included in that figure were the seven times Roundball I was grounded for repairs. In those games, the Pistons were 0-7.

Chances are whatever moves Davidson makes will be the right ones. Compared with the Pistons' owner, Midas had a copper touch. "I don't know if we're lucky or good," Davidson said. "Hopefully, you just use your head and figure things out. The more you do that, the luckier you become." ■

THE PLAYOFFS

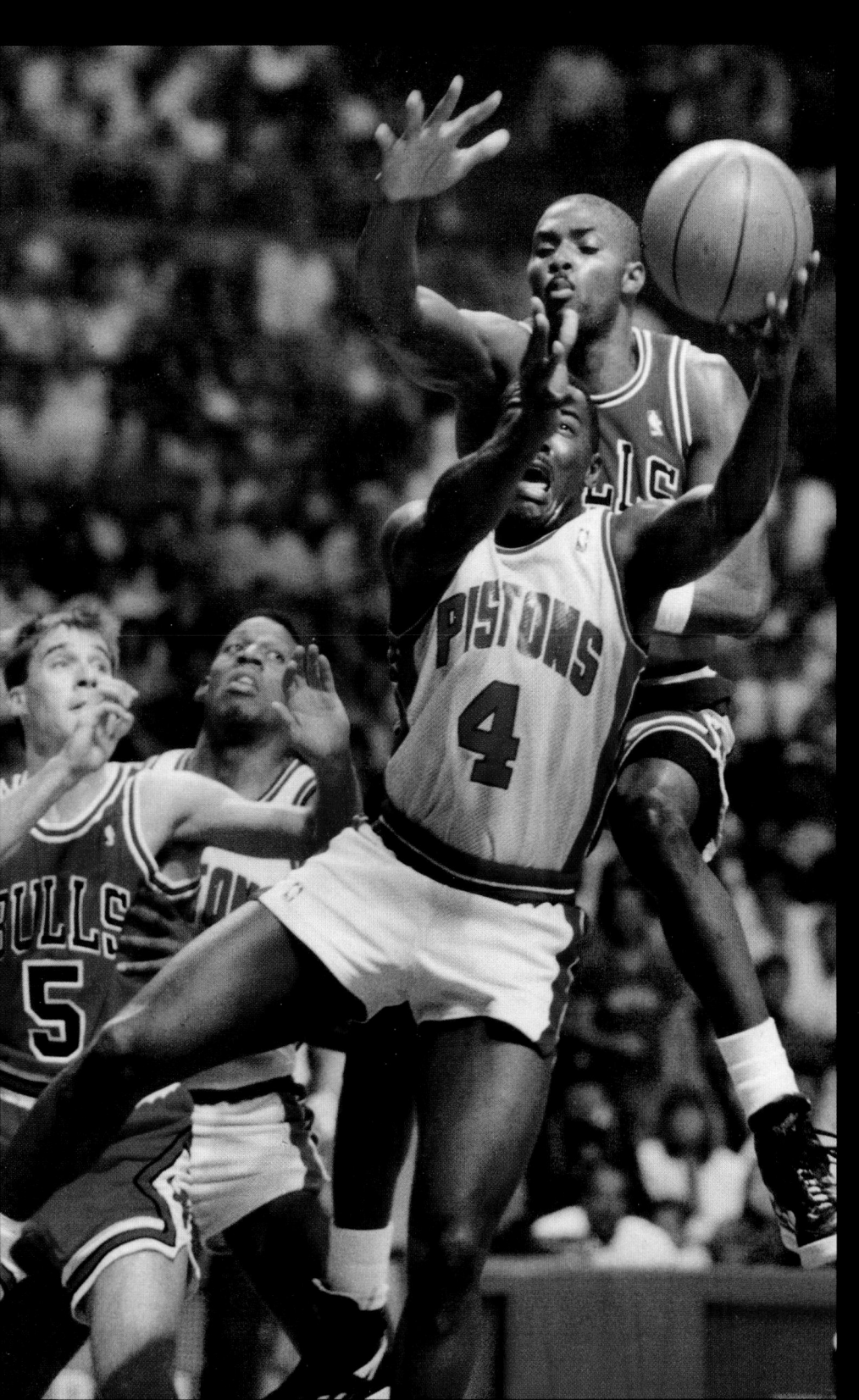

After winning 59 regular-season games, the Pistons stood 15 victories from their second straight title. Joe Dumars would help guard the crown through stops in Indianapolis, New York, Chicago and Portland

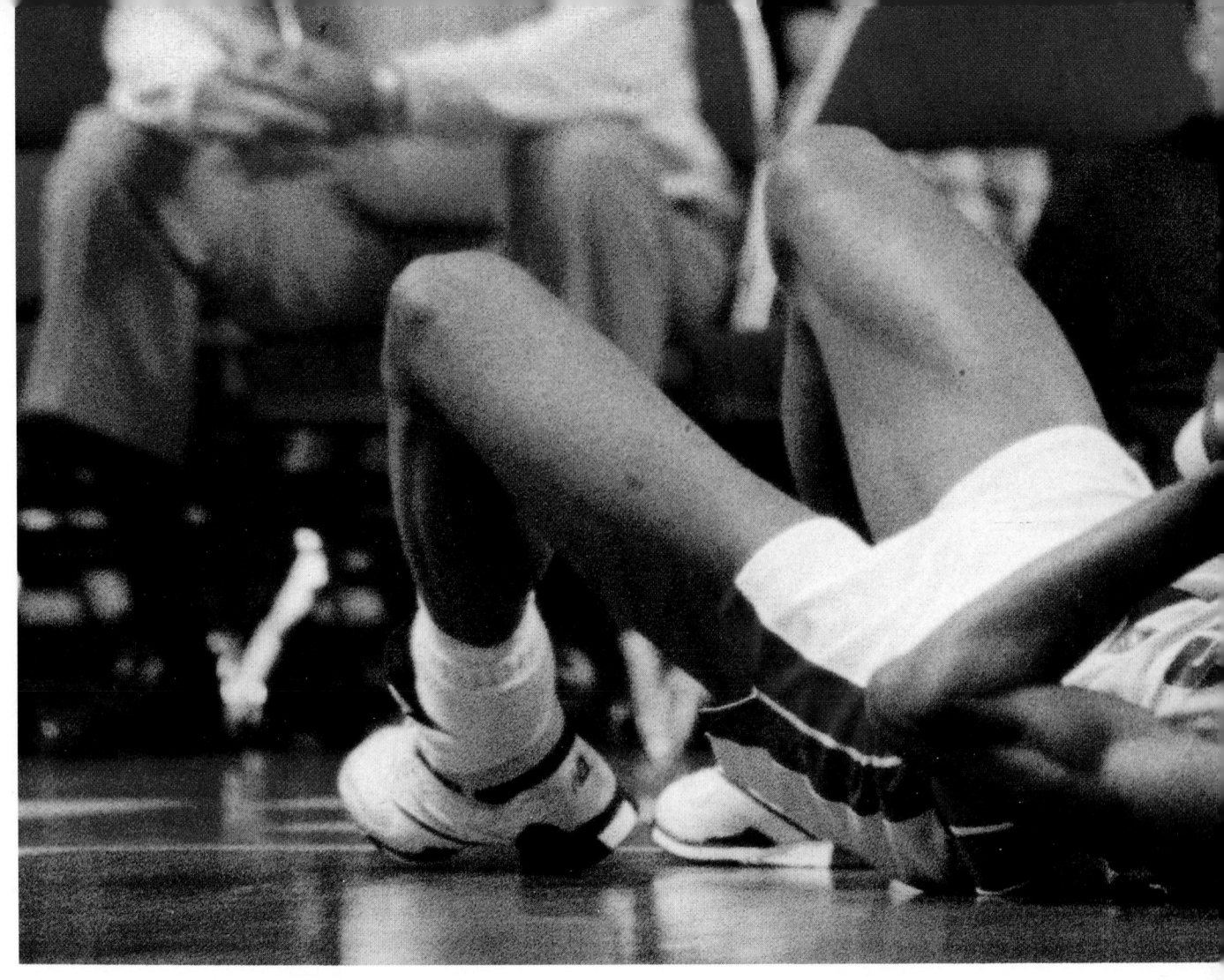

ROUND 1: INDIANA

By Mitch Albom

So there was Chuck Daly, standing in the hallway before the game, and a little kid in a Pacers jersey and yellow Pacers buttons sidled up next to him.

"You the Detroit coach?" he asked.

Daly said, "Yep."

And the kid said, "Don't beat us tonight, OK?"

Sorry, kid. Farewell, Indiana. Despite the dreams of this basketball state, the Pistons did to the Pacers May 1 in Indianapolis what any defending champ should do to a team still sucking from the playoff bottle: Put it to sleep and say good night. Sweep. See ya later.

"We came here to win," said Isiah Thomas, shrugging at the obvious after the Pistons won, 108-96, to advance to the second round of the playoffs. "We didn't come to enjoy the weather or see the sights, you know."

We know. So do the Pacers. The Pistons

grabbed this game by the neck in the second quarter, and tucked it away in the fourth. Thomas stole the ball and Dennis Rodman slammed the dunk and Bill Laimbeer threw in jumpers and that's it. Outta here. The Pistons were following one of the cardinal rules of the NBA: Never spend any more time in Indianapolis than you have to.

Of course, you can't tell that to a Hoosier.

Before tip-off, fans rocked Market Square Arena, cheering for their first playoff game in three years and only their third in a decade. Blue and yellow streamers hung from the rafters. Music blared. All the players were introduced. The crowd — perhaps showing playoff naivete — even stood and waved white handkerchiefs in support. Memo to Indiana: bad symbolism.

Not that it mattered. Surrender was obvious. Before Thomas singed the nets (23 points), before John Salley continued his spring blossom, before the Pistons tossed in eight points in 42 seconds to close the first half (three steals, three

The Not-So-Bad Boys had little trouble cutting down Detlef Schrempf and the rest of the Indiana big men.

lay-ups) this series was, for all intents and purposes, decided. No way Indiana gets a game against Detroit. Its day will come.

But not this year.

"Are you already finished thinking about the Pacers?" someone asked Joe Dumars just a few minutes after the victory. "We don't play them anymore, do we?" he said.

One down.

Daly had predicted "an all-out war" in this game. It never materialized.

Yes, there were double technicals called in the first minute of action, when Rodman and Detlef Schrempf did a little dance. But other than that, this was your basic basketball on basketball, which means the Pistons did it a little better, a lot deeper, and see ya later.

Balance? All but one Piston scored in double figures. Dumars earned his pay chasing Reggie Miller all night. Vinnie Johnson proved why he is an invaluable playoff weapon, coming alive during the fourth quarter. Salley continued his sudden gallop with 16 points in the first half. If he could learn to avoid fouls and hang onto rebounds instead of slapping them, he might get that $2.5 million contract on a silver platter.

Anyhow, in the end, all the noise, all the clamor, all the Pacers' home-court hype was doomed to fade. This is the difference between champions and wanna-be's. The latter desire it; the former get it done. So it was that during a loud and crazy fourth quarter, fans on their feet, waving, screaming, it was still the Pistons — particularly Thomas — making the key plays and getting the hoops, as calmly as though they were working in their basement.

"We don't get rattled by noise," the captain said. "We expect spurts like that. But we're an opportunistic team. If we were boxers, we'd be counterpunchers. We jab, jab, jab, wait. . . . " — he laughed — "and then we hit you real hard."

The Pacers don't wake up until October.

One down.

And three to go. The Pistons had forgotten Indianapolis by the time the plane left the runway. Next concern, Boston or New York. How many days' rest? What plays are gonna work? How late can we sleep tomorrow?

"Are we the first team to advance this soon?" Mark Aguirre had asked in the locker room afterward. When he was told yes, that's when he smiled. This is where defending champs take

The Pistons made forward Detlef Schrempf and guard Reggie Miller work for their points.

quiet pride. Doing it quickly. Getting to the real stage first.

It is a fascinating process, these NBA playoffs, like charting a singing career. You start on the Louisiana Hayride, you make it to the Grand Ole Opry, and one day, if you're really good, you play Carnegie Hall. You have to endure and learn from every level. It's a season unto itself, complete with slumps and injuries and heroes and momentum shifts.

The Pistons know this. The Pacers will learn it — maybe by the time that kid in the hallway grows to be a teenager.

The Pistons know that defense wins playoff games. And bench strength. And concentration. Want an example? Sometime during the second half of Game 1, Daly split his plants. Big hole. He never noticed. As the buzzer sounded, he was still screaming at the referees, underwear showing and everything.

The playoffs.

Daly put his experience in perspective: "After a while, all the hotel rooms and plane trips and arenas blend together. You just focus on the game at hand. There is no reason to look back in this league. . . . "

He paused and grinned. "Unless there's something back there that will help you win tonight."

Farewell, Indiana. Sorry, kid.

One down.

Next? ■

COMPOSITE BOX

Detroit (3-0)

PLAYER	G	MIN	FG	FT	REB	AST	PTS
Isiah Thomas	3	38.7	.488	.833	6.0	8.7	18.7
James Edwards	3	23.0	.472	.824	2.7	0.0	16.0
John Salley	3	29.7	.600	.750	6.3	1.0	16.0
Joe Dumars	3	34.3	.436	.857	0.7	4.3	15.3
Bill Laimbeer	3	37.3	.556	1.00	14.7	2.3	14.3
Vinnie Johnson	3	23.0	.448	.833	2.3	1.7	10.3
Mark Aguirre	3	25.3	.333	1.00	2.3	1.7	8.3
Dennis Rodman	3	28.3	.538	.200	6.0	1.7	5.0
William Bedford	1	1.0	.000	.000	0.0	0.0	0.0
TOTALS	**3**	**—**	**.482**	**.797**	**41.0**	**21.3**	**104.0**

Three-point goals: Thomas 4-5 (.800), Laimbeer 1-5 (.200), Dumars 0-1 (.000), Aguirre 0-2 (.000). Totals: 5-13 (.375).

Indiana (0-3)

PLAYER	G	MIN	FG	FT	REB	AST	PTS
Reggie Miller	3	41.7	.571	.905	4.0	2.0	20.7
Detlef Schrempf	3	41.7	.489	.938	7.3	1.7	20.3
Vern Fleming	3	37.7	.471	.889	4.3	6.0	13.3
Chuck Person	3	41.0	.378	.417	6.7	4.0	13.3
Rik Smits	3	32.0	.500	.818	5.3	1.0	12.3
LaSalle Thompson	3	18.0	.467	1.00	5.0	0.7	6.0
Mike Sanders	3	8.0	.455	.000	2.0	0.7	3.7
George McCloud	1	4.0	.500	.000	1.0	0.0	2.0
Calvin Natt	2	7.0	.333	.000	1.0	0.5	1.0
Rickey Green	3	10.3	.143	.000	0.3	1.0	0.7
Randy Wittman	2	5.5	.000	.000	0.5	0.0	0.0
TOTALS	**3**	**—**	**.461**	**.822**	**36.3**	**17.3**	**91.7**

Three-point goals: Sanders 1-1 (1.000), Miller 3-7 (.429), Person 1-10 (.100), Fleming 0-2 (.000), Schrempf 0-3 (.000). Totals: 5-23 (.235).

ROUND 2: NEW YORK

By Mitch Albom

After a while, you have seen all the games. The ones when you fall behind early, the ones when you blow them out, the ones when it seems you couldn't hit a basket if they put it at your knees. And deep down, if you are champions, you know the difference, even if the worried fans do not. This is the difference: You know the ones you can win, and you know when it's time to win them. It was time May 15 at the Palace. The New York Knicks were on the altar, their necks bare and vulnerable. It was the playoffs. It was the fourth quarter. It was time.

So the Pistons slapped themselves, toweled off the lethargy that had dragged them in the early part of the game, and did what champions do. Find the ball, no matter where it is, make it yours, and put it in. John Salley found it in Patrick Ewing's hands and stuffed it away, fell to the floor, and still poked it out for a fast break. Mark Aguirre found it with one man to beat and spun to the basket and dropped in a banker. Vinnie Johnson found it coming off glass and rose in the lane, Land Of The Giants, and grabbed it anyhow and put it in, two points, big lead.

Winning time. "I was yelling at them at halftime saying, 'OK, we're going back to New York, is that what you want? Another plane trip, more of that hotel food?' " said Chuck Daly, after his team rallied from a lousy start and captured Game 5 and the Eastern Conference semifinals, 95-84. No need to lecture, really, coach. Deep down, this Detroit team knew there would be no plane trip. The Pistons looked at the New York Knicks and saw a group that really wasn't ready to go further. The Knicks were tired. They were out of miracles. And the second half followed the script perfectly. Detroit played as though it had an appointment with destiny. New York played as though it had an appointment with the dentist.

"How happy are you that you won't have to see Patrick Ewing anymore?" someone asked Salley in the subdued but victorious locker room. "WHEW!" he yelled, breaking into a smile. "I told Charles Oakley he could stay at my house if he wanted to watch the next round. I didn't ask Patrick, because with all his money, he could buy

Bill Laimbeer & Co. stuffed Patrick Ewing in the opener — holding him to 19 points and four rebounds.

the house next to me if he wanted to watch the next round." Don't count on it. Ewing had enough of Detroit, especially after Game 5, when he scored just 22 points on 7-for-23 shooting. The defense wore him down almost as much as five games in seven days. He played every minute of the first three quarters. By the fourth, he was exhausted. He took baby steps up the court. Detroit had weathered Ewing's storm the best way a team can: Fire back with a lot of weapons.

Did we say a lot? Geez. It's like a lottery with these guys — you never know whose number is going to come up. Aguirre shoots out the lights? He leads the team with 25 points? Aguirre? Yes, he's a good player. But before Game 5, his best moment might have been shaking off Daly's suggestion that he go into Game 4, whispering instead, "Dennis is playing great. Leave him in."

But that's why the Pistons kill you. Aguirre sits quietly for the first four games, averages fewer than 19 minutes and only nine points, then scorches the Knicks, who were left wondering, "Where did this guy come from?" He was throwing them in from long range. From under the basket. He also played good defense and grabbed — are you ready? — eight rebounds. "We win as a team," he said, "and when you get hot on this team, the ball keeps coming to you."

Winning time. And so ends a weird — and sometimes wonderful — series. But it should have been expected. After all, the Pistons figured to play the Celtics, who had won two straight from New York — including the 157-128 record-setter in Game 2 — but lost the finale on their home court. In Game 1, the Pistons mauled the Knicks, 112-77 — New York's lowest playoff output in 34 years. How bad was it? In the fourth quarter, the Pistons actually led by 43. In Game 2,

Director Spike Lee caught the action, and Mark Aguirre caught the Knicks' ire.

James Edwards, the ageless Buddha, scored 21 first-half points and 32 overall. But Isiah Thomas had to score 11 of Detroit's last 12 points, including a trio of three-pointers, for a 104-97 victory, the Pistons' 12th straight in the playoffs — only one behind the 1988-89 Lakers' record.

But then came Game 3. Ewing went nuts — 45 points, 16 rebounds, six assists. And the Pistons went cold — from the free-throw line. Missed 14 times. Only 21-for-35. Final: Knicks 111, Pistons 103. Game 4? The weirdest of all. Ewing went the entire first half without a point. In his building, before he even broke a sweat, Ewing got whistled for an offensive foul. Four minutes later, he got whistled for another. He sat for the rest of the first quarter, came back in to start the second and — squeeek! — got called for another foul within nine seconds. Referee Jack Madden should be nominated for the Congressional Medal of Honor. Weird? Joe Dumars sat for seven long minutes down the stretch — why? who knows why? — then came off the bench and scored the Pistons' last 13 points. Final: Pistons 102, Knicks

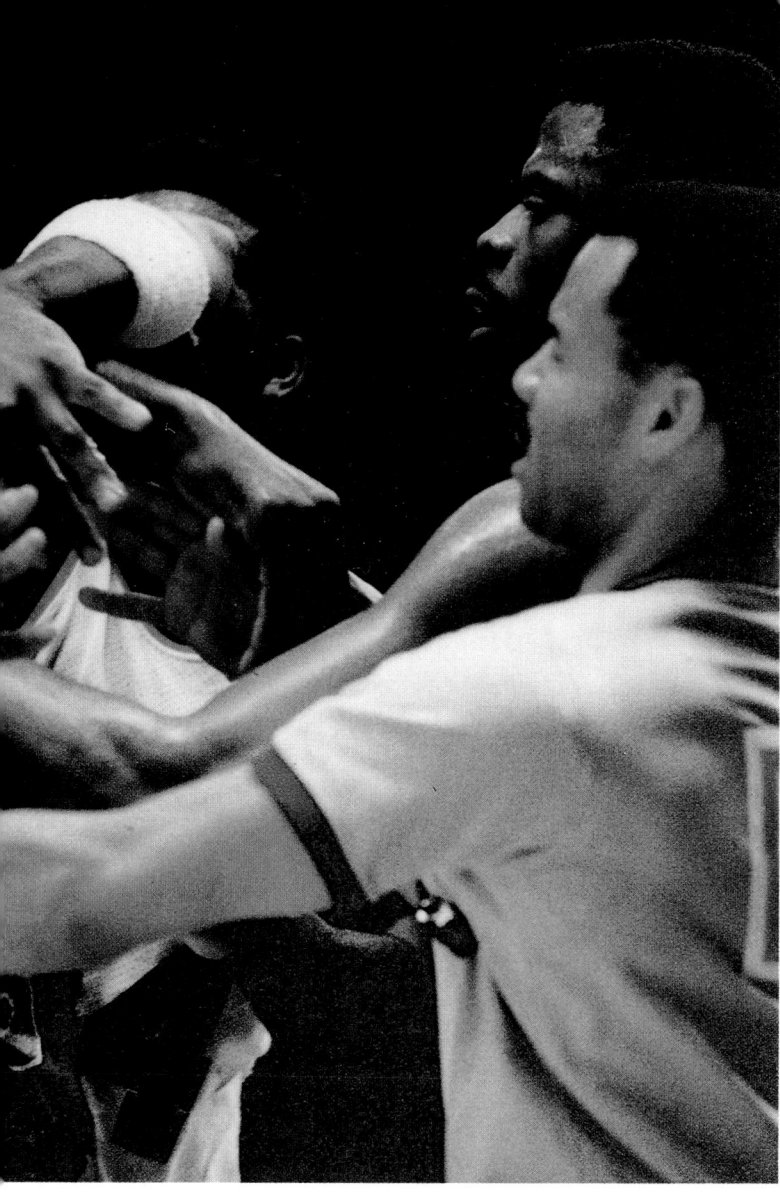

90. Up 3-1, the series was all but in the bag.

Winning time. And on go the Pistons, to the Eastern Conference finals for the fourth year in a row. We should realize how unique this group is, all arms and legs and swarming defense, not really caring who gets the basket. "They can score 80 points and beat you convincingly," said New York's Kenny Walker. That's high praise.

And you know the best part? Their attitude. Before the game, Edwards was throwing away his sneakers, the magic sneakers, the ones he had worn when the series began. Before the game? When many players on a streak wouldn't dare change anything? "Too loose," he said nonchalantly. "I don't like 'em too loose."

"But those are historic," someone protested. "You set your career playoff high in those sneakers. You've outdueled Ewing in them."

"Well, I'll have to get another pair," he said, laughing, without looking up. "I'm not superstitious like that."

He signed the old shoes, handed them to the ball boy, and broke open a new box. A few hours later, as the fourth quarter ticked away, Edwards leaped, in his new shoes, and stuffed Ewing. And you can bet it never occurred to him. When you think like a champion, it is only the sum that matters, not the parts. ∎

James Edwards had a big hand in helping the Pistons clinch for the first time at the Palace. They had ended five straight series on the road.

COMPOSITE BOX

Pistons (4-1)

PLAYER	G	MIN	FG%	FT%	REB	AST	PTS
James Edwards	5	29.0	.588	.708	2.6	0.6	19.4
Isiah Thomas	5	36.2	.438	.765	4.4	8.4	18.4
Joe Dumars	5	36.0	.458	.913	2.8	5.8	15.0
Mark Aguirre	5	18.8	.560	.500	4.2	1.4	12.4
Vinnie Johnson	5	22.8	.529	.500	2.8	3.0	11.2
Bill Laimbeer	5	31.8	.468	1.00	10.0	1.0	10.0
John Salley	5	23.4	.393	.692	6.0	1.4	8.0
Dennis Rodman	5	34.0	.581	.333	10.6	1.0	7.6
William Bedford	1	7.0	.250	.000	2.0	0.0	2.0
Scott Hastings	1	5.0	1.00	.000	0.0	0.0	2.0
David Greenwood	2	9.5	1.00	.000	0.0	0.0	1.0
Gerald Henderson	2	6.0	.000	.000	1.0	2.0	0.0
TOTALS	5	—	.501	.703	44.2	23.4	103.2

Three-point goals: Johnson 1-1 (1.000), Laimbeer 5-11 (.455), Thomas 9-23 (.391), Aguirre 1-6 (.167), Dumars 0-1 (.000). Totals: 16-42 (.381).

Knicks (1-4)

PLAYER	G	MIN	FG%	FT%	REB	AST	PTS
Patrick Ewing	5	37.2	.466	.952	9.6	2.2	27.2
Maurice Cheeks	5	36.8	.463	1.00	4.6	8.2	12.6
Gerald Wilkins	5	32.4	.435	.875	2.8	4.0	12.2
Charles Oakley	5	37.6	.500	.636	12.6	2.6	11.2
Kiki Vandeweghe	5	24.2	.394	.875	1.0	1.8	7.6
Eddie Wilkins	3	9.0	.500	.286	3.3	0.0	5.3
Johnny Newman	5	20.0	.308	.667	1.4	0.8	5.2
Mark Jackson	5	9.0	.444	.625	0.8	1.8	4.2
Trent Tucker	5	18.2	.333	1.00	1.4	1.2	4.2
Brian Quinnett	1	9.0	.500	.000	7.0	2.0	3.0
Kenny Walker	5	16.4	.467	.500	2.0	0.6	3.0
Stuart Gray	1	5.0	.333	.000	3.0	0.0	2.0
TOTALS	5	—	.439	.795	40.2	23.8	91.8

Three-point goals: Quinnett 1-1 (1.000), Vandeweghe 5-10 (.500), Tucker 3-9 (.333), Newman 1-4 (.250), Wilkins 0-4 (.000), Cheeks 0-2 (.000), Ewing 0-1 (.000), Jackson 0-1 (.000). Totals: 10-32 (.313).

CHICAGO: GAMES 1 & 2

By Corky Meinecke

Chicago Bulls guard Michael Jordan, whose nickname is Air, let off a little steam at the Palace after his team fell behind, 2-0, in the Eastern Conference finals. Make that a *lot* of steam. Jordan kicked folding chairs and had several harsh words for his teammates at halftime, then rushed to the team bus without speaking to reporters only moments after the Pistons had completed their 102-93 victory in Game 2 on May 22.

The Bulls couldn't corral Vinnie Johnson in Game 2. The Pistons caught Michael Jordan in a defensive vise. He shot 39.5 percent for Games 1 and 2.

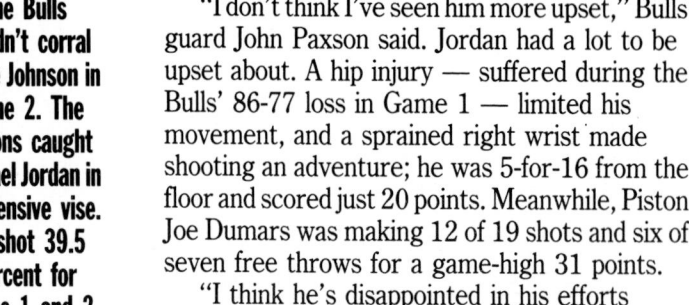

"I don't think I've seen him more upset," Bulls guard John Paxson said. Jordan had a lot to be upset about. A hip injury — suffered during the Bulls' 86-77 loss in Game 1 — limited his movement, and a sprained right wrist made shooting an adventure; he was 5-for-16 from the floor and scored just 20 points. Meanwhile, Piston Joe Dumars was making 12 of 19 shots and six of seven free throws for a game-high 31 points.

"I think he's disappointed in his efforts tonight," Bulls coach Phil Jackson said. "For 14 minutes he played pretty good basketball. But other than that, he really didn't show the characteristics he's shown all year."

Nothing angered Jordan more than the Bulls' 14 turnovers by halftime. Those — coupled with 35 percent shooting — were primarily responsible for the Pistons' 53-38 lead at that point. "He didn't mention names; he was just so disappointed," said Bulls forward Horace Grant. "I can't blame him. Some guys don't know what the playoffs are all about. The guys know who they are. They've got to be more physical."

Jordan's blistering halftime speech prompted a 24-9 third-quarter run, but the Bulls didn't have anything left after Craig Hodges' jumper gave them a 67-66 lead with 3:34 left in the quarter. The Pistons regained control, scoring eight of the last 10 points in the quarter, as Jordan seemed to fade out of the picture. "He definitely wasn't the Jordan we're used to," said Vinnie Johnson, who had 18 points and eight rebounds in 29 minutes. "He wasn't aggressive. He wasn't going after the ball. He seemed like he was trying to get his teammates involved."

It didn't work.

Nor did it work in Game 1 on May 20, when the Bulls also failed to pick up where their superstar guard left off. Jordan, who bruised his left hip when he fell while shooting late in the first quarter, scored just nine fewer points than the total scored by all his teammates, 43-34. He shot 44 percent; they shot 35 percent. He made eight free throws; they made three. He committed one turnover; they committed 14. "As a unit," Hodges said, "we can't play much worse."

As a unit, the Pistons didn't play much better. Not counting Dumars, who led the team with 27 points, Detroit shot 37 percent. "Just give us one hot guy," said Bill Laimbeer, nodding in Dumars' direction. "One hot guy. That's all we need."

In the Bulls' case, that was all they had. ∎

CHICAGO: GAMES 3 & 4

By Mitch Albom

This was as bad as the Pistons would play all season. There was Bill Laimbeer, on his Lost Weekend, doing little more than taking up space. There was James Edwards, facing free throws as if they were a firing squad. And there was John Salley, collecting fouls as if they were berries. There were the Chicago Bulls, embarrassing the Pistons at their own game, with a defense that was glove-tight, stealing and blocking and scoring until they had won Game 4 on May 28 at Chicago Stadium, 108-101, tying the Eastern Conference finals at two victories apiece.

You wanted to take the Pistons and smack them on their mittens. You wanted to tell them, "Come on. You're old enough to know better than this." Here they were, coming off a 107-102 loss in Game 3 on May 26, telling everybody how focused they would be in the next game — and then out they come as if they forgot to take their Walkmans off. "How does something like this happen, after you all said your concentration would be better?" someone asked Joe Dumars in the suddenly hard-edged locker room. "It's a good question," he said. "And I wish I could give you a long, thoughtful answer. But I can't."

All right, let's try: After Game 3, no Piston seemed concerned that the Bulls had won. The Pistons said they needed only to play better to win. They came to the arena for Game 4 relaxed and sure of themselves. The answer lies in attitude, hunger, concentration. And the answer lies in the past. Go back to when Boston was the perennial conference champion, and Detroit was the hungry challenger. The Celtics figured their experience would always win it; it always had. But season by season, game by game, the Pistons crept up their backs, until finally, one year, they strangled them.

You want to know the scariest thing about the Bulls' success in Games 3 and 4? They looked like the Pistons. "It's been a long time since we had that type of game against Detroit," said a smiling Michael Jordan, who bombed away for 47 points in Game 3 and stuck in the knife once again with 42 points and tenacious defense in Game 4. "We played the whole game with intensity. Our

defense was the best it's been. We showed maturity; we showed poise; we showed concentration." All the things Detroit lacked.

Which is why Detroit looked anemic for the first half, during which it missed 12 straight shots. And why, at one point, the Pistons had twice as many turnovers as baskets. And why Salley picked up two fouls in eight seconds, which is fast, even for him. And why Mark Aguirre played all of nine minutes, in which he 1) turned the ball over, 2) had a shot blocked, 3) committed an offensive foul, 4) turned the ball over, 5) took a seat and did not return until the game's final seconds.

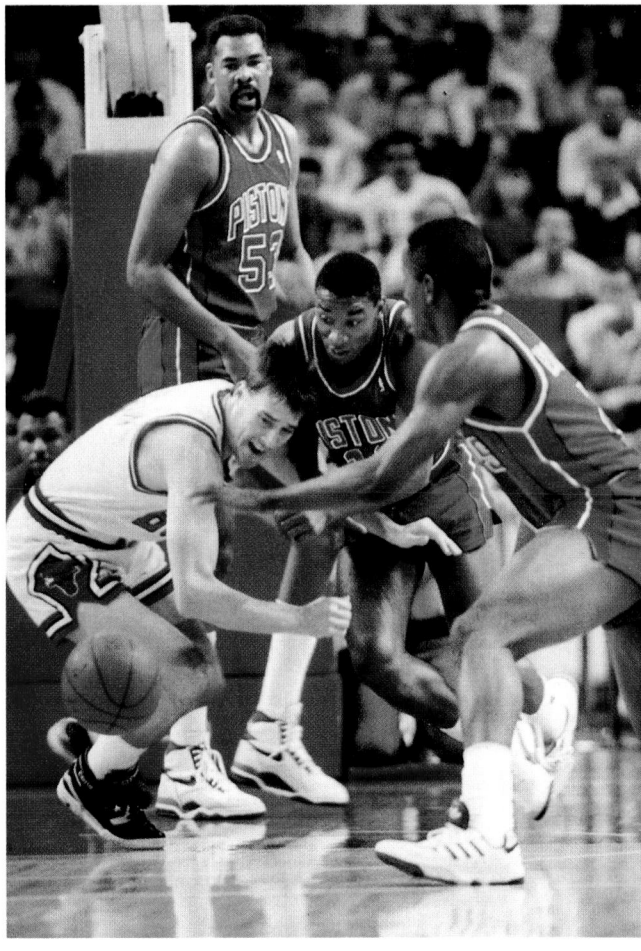

Horace Grant and John Paxson kept Isiah Thomas and Company on the run in Chicago, where Thomas had 62 points for Games 3 and 4.

The Bulls — not the Pistons — were the defensive gems. And through that defense, and Jordan's basket-per-minute in the fourth quarter, they maintained the poise to keep the lead. Detroit was a better team than Chicago, with better talent and more experience, and so it was expected to win. But expectations do not put the ball in the basket. "Maybe we've had things too easy," coach Chuck Daly mused. "Our club hasn't been backed against the wall all year. Every team wants what we have. We own the title. It's up to us to decide how badly we want to keep it." ■

CHICAGO: GAME 5

By Mitch Albom

The faces said it all: Mark Aguirre in a primal scream. Chuck Daly hollering with his eyes squeezed shut. John Salley in a monster grimace, rising above the crowd, the emperor of the air, grabbing the basketball and squeezing it until it seemed sure to pop. "Ours!" they all seemed to be yelling. The ball is ours. The game is ours. This battle in this head-knocking war is ours.

"I think we have gotten the kinks out," Aguirre said in a dead-serious tone after his hot shooting helped spark Detroit past Chicago, 97-83, May 30 for a 3-2 series lead. "What you saw tonight was the Detroit Pistons."

Particularly those who had been deemed missing in Chicago. Aguirre, who played only nine minutes in Game 4, did yeoman duty in Game 5, dropping 8-of-10 shots for 19 points, most in the fourth quarter. Bill Laimbeer, woeful in Chicago, rediscovered his shooting, as did fellow big man James Edwards. Salley, foul-plagued in previous games, played possibly the most effective eight-point game ever, grabbing 10 rebounds.

"They were feeling too good about themselves," Edwards said. "We had to show them that we're still the world champions and they still have to beat us." They did it by breaking the Chicago press. They did it by boxing out for rebounds. They did it with the bench taking over, scoring 35 points and playing as many minutes as most starters. And they did it in crunch time, the fourth quarter, when, behind a delightful thunder from the sellout crowd, they twisted the vise and watched the Bulls turn blue. Every shot was met with two hands up. Every rebound was challenged with full torsos. Every pass to Michael Jordan brought a cavalry of defenders — all that was missing were the trumpets. Mr. Miracle was held to 22 points. And Detroit outscored Chicago, 25-19, in the fourth quarter.

The game had a hard edge from start to finish, and for good reason. The Pistons had taken a blow broadside in Chicago, and they wore the scars. Joe Dumars had a cut inside his upper lip the size of a pea, suffered in Game 4. He could feel it on every play, the blood dripping onto his tongue. Dennis Rodman had a sore ankle from Game 4, too. He felt it on every run, the throb, the swelling. Edwards had a cut above his eye; he was pressing gauze to stop the bleeding. Laimbeer had a gash in his pride, his shooting touch having

The Pistons — and their crowd — were plenty bad in Game 5. Mark Aguirre drove for 19 points. John Salley soared for great defense and 10 rebounds.

left him ineffective. Nobody was forgetting. Nobody could. Hard edge? You bet. For the first time since winning the 1989 title, the Pistons were backed into a corner. This is how they responded: Rodman dunk. Salley block. Dumars swish. Aguirre for three. "You have to protect your home turf," said Dumars, who scored 20 points and made Jordan sweat on defense. "Bad things happen when you lose at home."

Now back to Chicago. ∎

CHICAGO: GAME 6

By Mitch Albom

So there was another bullet in the chamber after all. The Bulls fired, the Pistons went down, leaving 48 minutes of basketball war to determine who gets off the ground and who stays there until the fall. Seventh Hell. Who needs this?

Not the Pistons, who discovered the nickname Windy City really means you never know which way the Bulls are going to blow. Cold and tired — as they did in Detroit in Game 5 — or hot and deadly, as they did June 1 in Game 6. The bad news: Detroit lost. The worse news: It was more than Michael Jordan this time. It was Scottie Pippen pulling up inside and burying shots, and Horace Grant grabbing rebounds as if they came with bonus money, and Craig Hodges, who had been shooting so terribly in this series you could count his baskets on one hand, suddenly finding the bottom of the net and dumping the Pistons there as well. Oh, yeah. Jordan had 29, that's all.

Seventh Hell.

"We are more driven than ever to win this thing," Jordan yelled after the Bulls demolished the Pistons, 109-91, to force a Game 7 showdown at the Palace for the Eastern Conference title. "We are going to Detroit with a clear mind. All bets are off. We did the job."

No argument there. The Bulls would not budge. Not this time. Never mind that this was the one-year anniversary of their playoff departure of 1989, courtesy of the Pistons. New year, new story. This time, the defending champions did not even raise a shiver from the Chicago men. But then, the Pistons didn't really play like defending champions, either.

"We shoulda won, we shoulda won," Dennis Rodman kept repeating in the locker room, his swollen left ankle throbbing with pain. "We can't keep talking about experience in a seventh game. We had all the experience in the world tonight, and we still didn't do it."

You can say that again. Missed shots? You don't want to know. Bench production? The Pistons' subs were uncharacteristically smoked. Vinnie Johnson missed all 10 of his shots. Defense? This might have been the most depressing part of all. For much of the night, the

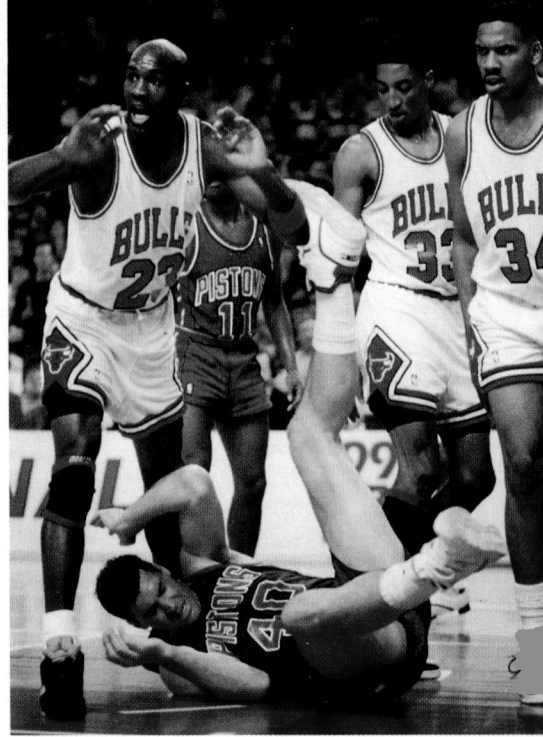

With their backs to the wall, the Bulls put Bill Laimbeer on his.

offense consisted of a few spins and a dump back to the top of the key. Nobody could drive. Nobody could take a good shot. Balls slammed off the side of the backboard. After Game 4, Isiah Thomas defended his team, saying the Bulls simply outplayed the Pistons. But in Game 6, the Pistons were making their own mistakes. They were losing — and Jordan wasn't even breathing hard.

How do you explain that third quarter, when almost everything the Pistons threw up looked like something, well, they threw up? Six baskets? Twenty-four tries? Five full minutes without a field goal? Meanwhile, the Bulls, smelling the kill, gave the ball to Jordan, and he hung in the air until all the Pistons came down, then bang, bang, bang, bang, bang. He scored 18 points in little more

Pistons were a step slow, flailing, scrambling. The Bulls beat them with the pass; they buried open shots. If champions revert to form when threatened, well, where was the Detroit form? The Pistons played three games in Chicago Stadium and did not look like themselves in any of them. And the Bulls looked like Giants.

It is time to ask a serious question: Can a building really do this? Turn a championship team into a slower, less accurate, less concentrated version of itself — three times in one week? Or are the Bulls getting that much better with each game? "They broke us down," said James Edwards, who had a depressing night, scoring 12 points and picking up five fouls. "They broke down our defense."

Chicago was one explosion after another — a fitting description for the arena as well. Pistons fans could sense at any moment the game could fly away, gone on the wings of Bulls euphoria. They had to be scared in the second quarter, when, with Jordan resting, the Bulls opened an 11-point lead. The Pistons looked confused; their

Bulls forward Horace Grant celebrated. Isiah Thomas, Joe Dumars and Bill Laimbeer could only watch glumly as Game 6 slipped away.

than eight minutes. It ain't the shoes.

One more game. Who has the advantage? There is every kind of theory: 1) The Pistons. It's their home court. 2) The Bulls. They have the momentum. 3) The Pistons. They have experience. 4) The Bulls. They have nothing to lose. About the only thing the Pistons can be certain about is that they won't have to see Chicago Stadium anymore. Trying to win there is like trying to douse a five-alarm fire with a garden hose. And this Chicago fire was hot enough already. Seventh Hell. Somebody burns. ■

CHICAGO: GAME 7

By Mitch Albom

In the end, that wasn't just a basketball, that was a message slamming through those Palace nets: John Salley hammering home an alley-oop, then spinning with the look of a killer. Bill Laimbeer banging home a lay-up, coming down with his fists clenched. Mark Aguirre waiting for Michael Jordan to get close, then windmilling one in his face. The Palace fans rose in a thunderous roar. They understood, and so did the Bulls. Here was the message: Enough already. Our building. Our defense. You go home. We go on.

Finally, Finals.

"I said to myself, 'I'm not smiling, I'm not grinning, I'm not laughing today,' " said an exhausted Salley, after the Pistons choked the Bulls in the biggest basketball game in a long time, 93-74, to win the Eastern Conference finals in Game 7 and advance to the promised land. "Even the coaches said to me, 'Lighten up.' But I said, 'Nuh-uh. Not until I see 00:00 on the clock.' " Lighten up? Who could lighten up? It was a leaden June 3 afternoon, filled with dark omens and nasty ghosts and voices, all these voices saying, "Don't lose it. You can't lose it. Not after all you've accomplished." This is what it's like to be defending NBA champion. You have to battle your reputation as well as your opponent.

In the 12th meeting of the season between these rivals, the Pistons were up to both. It was hardly a beautiful game, but it was bodies slamming and bodies jamming and bodies fighting in midair for free balls. It was Isiah Thomas driving in, then dishing off to wide-open teammates. It was Salley playing larger than life — and he's pretty big to begin with — blocking five shots and sparking a second quarter that broke Chicago's spirit.

Mostly, as usual, it was defense, three Pistons rising with every Jordan levitation, three Pistons rising with every defensive rebound. No surprise that the loudest crowd noise on this very loud afternoon came when the Pistons set up not to score but to defend; fans know where Detroit's bread is buttered. "They overwhelmed us," Jordan said, which is exactly what you should do to a one-man army. And when the buzzer sounded, and the crowd sang the NA-NA-HEY-HEY song, the Pistons raced past Jordan, the best basketball player on the planet, slapped his hand and kept on going. You're the king, but we're the champs. See ya in November.

Finally, Finals.

How long was this series? A month? A year? It seemed as if Detroit's entire schedule was against the Chicago Bulls. Every time the Pistons brought the ball up, the Bulls shouted out the play. Every time Jordan eyeballed his teammates, the Pistons yelled out his intentions. It was like watching two grizzly bears in a broom closet. They couldn't avoid each other even if they wanted to. Maybe that's why this thing went seven games, with each team winning its home games. So close are they, Chicago and Detroit, that crowd noise can make a difference. Maybe that's it. Or maybe it's something else, a pride thing for the champions that needed the threat of extinction to bring it to life. In Game 6, the Pistons were at their lowest point, blown out in Chicago, down to one game, hearing whispers.

"And then this funny thing happened," Salley said. "We got stuck at the Chicago airport when our plane was damaged. We had to hang around in this lounge for an hour or so waiting. It's longer

Isiah Thomas got nothing but leather on this Michael Jordan drive. Joe Dumars, despite a pulled groin, also hounded Jordan, who scored 31 points.

than we usually stay together after a game. We started talking, you know, about where we were and what we had to do." By the time they touched down in the wee hours, the directive was clear: Remember who we are. "The better team," Thomas insisted. And Salley might have been listening more than anyone else. When he entered late in the first quarter, the score was tied; by the time he left, the game was Detroit's for the taking. This was the Spider Man: block Jordan, block Horace Grant, block Ed Nealy, slam a basket off a Thomas dish, swish a jumper with the shot clock at one second, makes a great pass to Aguirre for a lay-up and — get this — drives the length of the court for a basket and a foul. Salley? The length of the court? "Hey, you know how many guys I'd have to beat up if we had lost this game?" he joked afterward. "This whole room. No way we were losing."

No matter what it took. And it took all they had — holding Chicago to the lowest playoff output in the Pistons' history. Make no mistake. This is a difficult Bulls team, growing stronger and more confident with every playoff battle. They were playing without injured guard John Paxson, on a foreign court, with everyone but Jordan shooting a collective 24 percent. And they still didn't die until the fourth quarter. There were moments where you wondered whether Jordan (31 points) really could win a series all by himself. In the end the answer was no. "It was not

meant to be," he admitted, sadly. "It's tough to lose as a leader. It's my job to show the other guys how to relax and stay calm, but some of them still didn't play as well as they're capable. . . . Detroit proved they're the better team on paper. And the better team on the court."

Nice. Classy. You have to admire Jordan, who for several years has tried to drag his team single-handedly to the finals. He is getting closer. But like Sisyphus, he seems doomed to roll the boulder up the mountain, only to see it roll back down. As a fan, you feel sorry for him. But that's as a fan. "Sympathy?" Joe Dumars said, responding to a question. He grinned. He hobbled back a step. His right thigh was wrapped in a

COMPOSITE BOX

Pistons (4-3)

PLAYER	G	MIN	FG%	FT%	REB	AST	PTS
Joe Dumars	7	37.3	.500	.846	2.0	3.6	20.0
Isiah Thomas	7	38.4	.396	.833	6.1	8.6	17.6
Mark Aguirre	7	21.3	.548	.929	6.4	1.6	12.0
James Edwards	7	26.3	.452	.433	4.4	0.9	9.9
John Salley	7	28.0	.531	.814	5.1	1.1	9.9
Dennis Rodman	7	32.3	.595	.700	9.7	0.6	9.1
Bill Laimbeer	7	29.3	.403	.750	7.1	0.6	9.0
Vinnie Johnson	7	23.9	.345	.810	3.6	4.0	8.3
William Bedford	3	3.7	.000	1.00	0.0	0.0	0.7
Scott Hastings	2	3.5	.000	.000	0.0	0.0	0.0
Gerald Henderson	4	1.3	.000	.000	0.3	0.0	0.0
TOTALS	7	—	.455	.767	44.7	20.9	96.0

Three-point goals: Aguirre 3-8 (.375), Thomas 8-24 (.333), Dumars 3-10 (.300), Johnson 1-5 (.200), Laimbeer 1-5 (.200), Hastings 0-2 (.000), Henderson 0-3 (.000). Totals: 16-57 (.281).

Bulls (3-4)

PLAYER	G	MIN	FG%	FT%	REB	AST	PTS
Michael Jordan	7	42.3	.467	.875	7.1	6.3	32.1
Scottie Pippen	7	40.9	.426	.750	6.3	3.7	16.6
Horace Grant	7	38.1	.408	.792	11.7	2.4	11.6
Bill Cartwright	7	26.9	.404	.667	4.3	1.1	7.1
John Paxson	6	23.5	.378	1.00	1.3	2.7	6.7
Craig Hodges	7	19.3	.341	.500	1.1	1.3	5.3
Stacey King	7	15.4	.321	.850	1.7	0.4	5.0
B.J. Armstrong	7	15.4	.263	.917	1.6	1.4	4.4
Ed Nealy	7	15.9	.389	.636	3.1	0.3	3.0
Charles Davis	1	2.0	1.00	.000	1.0	0.0	2.0
Will Perdue	7	5.3	.400	.833	1.1	0.3	1.9
Jeff Sanders	1	1.0	.000	.000	0.0	0.0	0.0
TOTALS	7	—	.407	.811	39.4	19.6	93.0

Three-point goals: Paxson 4-7 (.571), Pippen 6-20 (.300), Hodges 8-28 (.286), Jordan 6-21 (.286), Grant 0-2 (.000), Armstrong 0-3 (.000). Totals: 24-81 (.296).

bandage. The cut in his mouth — courtesy of two elbows — was still unhealed. He had the look of a man who had just worked triple shifts at the plant. And Jordan is his friend. "I like him," Dumars said. "I admire him. But sympathy? I don't have any sympathy for him." Or as Salley put it: "He's from Mars? Let him go back to Mars. We got things to do." Wait a minute. Finals? For the third straight year the Pistons reached the glory round. In less than 48 hours, the Trail Blazers would walk out on the Palace floor and a whole new war would begin. Odd, wasn't it? So intense was this Chicago series, you almost forgot it was for the right to go on, not to go home a champion.

Finally, Finals. ■

The noisy Palace fans didn't do anything to help Scottie Pippen's migraine headaches. He missed nine of 10 shots and scored only two points.

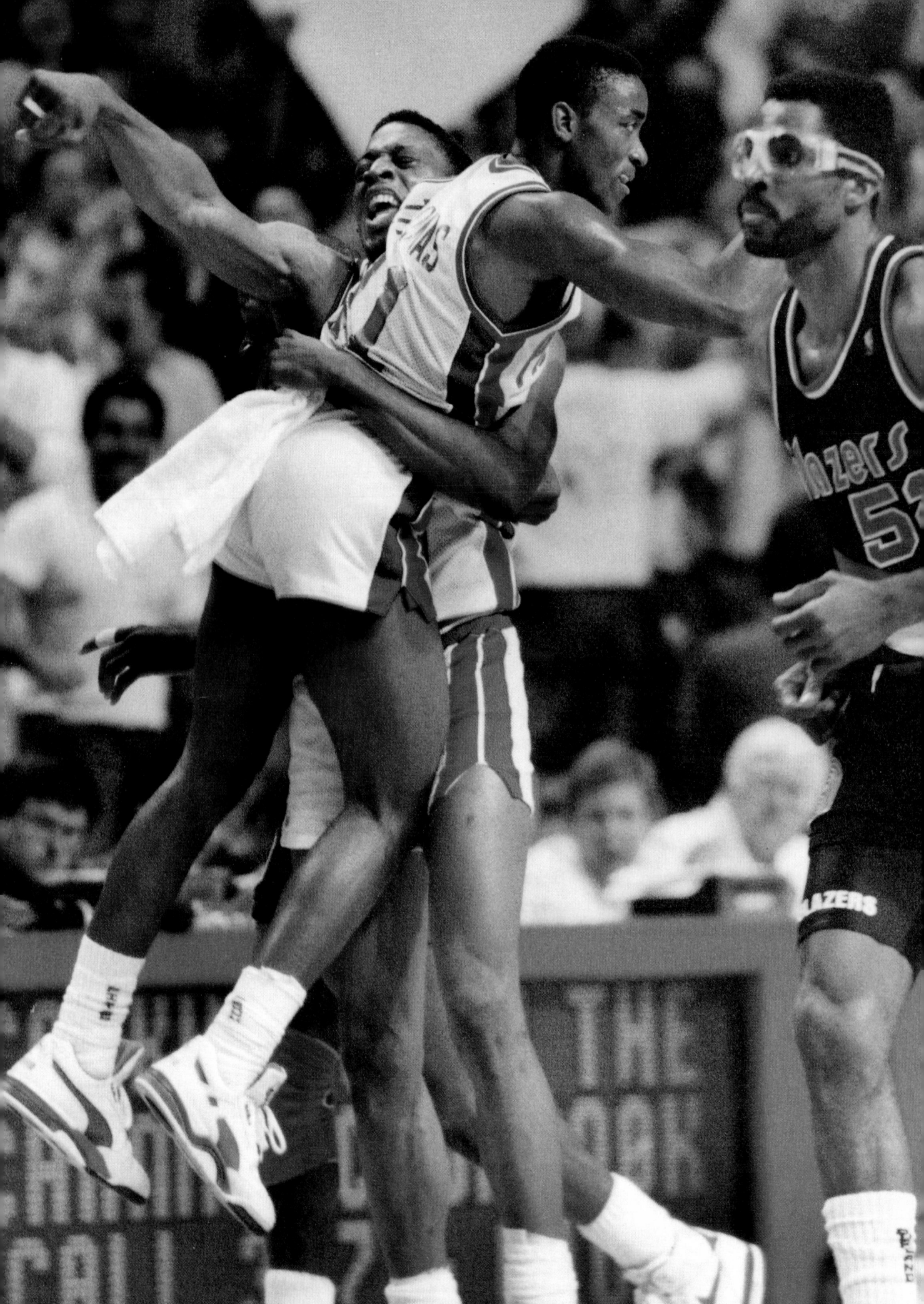

PORTLAND: GAME 1

By Mitch Albom

Late in the game, with the score tied and the crowd on its feet, Chuck Daly leaned toward his captain and snapped an ammonia capsule under his nose. Isiah Thomas jerked his head as if someone had slapped him across the cheek. The message was clear: Wake up.

Message received.

"I've used those capsules before," Thomas said, laughing, after leading a furious rally that gave Game 1 of the NBA Finals to the defending champions, 105-99. "But usually it's on some night in New Jersey, middle of the winter, when there's like 5,000 people in the stands and you're just trying to stay awake."

Whatever works. Suddenly, after an evening of near sleepwalking, the Pistons were back in control, with Thomas clanging the breakfast bell. In the final seven minutes, the little giant fired away — jumper, lay-up, jumper, three-pointer — scoring 12 of the Pistons' last 16 points. Dennis Rodman, John Salley and Bill Laimbeer built a fort around the Portland offense. The Palace fans were at their most intimidating, making noise like a jet engine and prompting Buck Williams and Jerome Kersey to miss four crucial free throws.

"Hey, we didn't think you guys were gonna get here in time," the crowd seemed to gush as their heroes walked off the court, victorious. "Glad you showed up."

Before this June 5 game, Thomas spoke of the advantage the Trail Blazers had in the series opener: "The pressure is on the home team in the first game. If they play their cards right, they could win this thing."

For much of the night it seemed they would. The Blazers were quicker than Detroit, a few inches higher, closer to the basketball and definitely on the right side of the referee's whistle. Williams was rising and throwing in jumpers, and Clyde Drexler was driving to the hoop and dropping in baskets, and Kevin Duckworth was swishing one-handers from the outside. The Blazers looked like a lay-up machine.

And the Pistons? They . . . were . . . moving . . . in . . . slow . . . motion. After three quarters, they were shooting 36 percent. "In the finals," Salley said, "the body is nothing without the head." And this body was headless. These weren't bombs Detroit was missing. Try lay-ups, turnarounds in the paint. Try dropped passes and

After carrying the Pistons down the stretch, Isiah Thomas got a lift from Dennis Rodman. But Thomas insisted on sharing credit with Mark Aguirre, whose 18 points kept Detroit within rally range.

missed cues and guys out of sync on defense. It was like one of those dreams in which you're falling and falling and at the last second you wake up. Fortunately, Thomas (33 points) touched earth first. Once there, he seemed to race around the court, slapping his teammates in the face. "You up? You up?"

Wake up and smell the victory.

"It's will, not skill," Thomas said to a mob of reporters. They nodded. They scribbled. But most wanted to know about that fourth quarter. Sixteen points? Those rainbow jumpers. "What does it feel like? How do you do it? When do you know you've got it?"

They are the questions of people who have never watched Thomas. He does this all the time. This time it happened to be in front of the whole country. "We're a team," he said. "This game was decided by who wanted it more, that's all. When we came out after that time-out (down by 10, with 7:05 left), I just went around to each of our guys and said, 'How badly do you want it?' "

He then went out and gave them his answer. Now let's be honest: There were many times during this game when Isiah tried to do it all and came up short. His shots clanked; his passes were

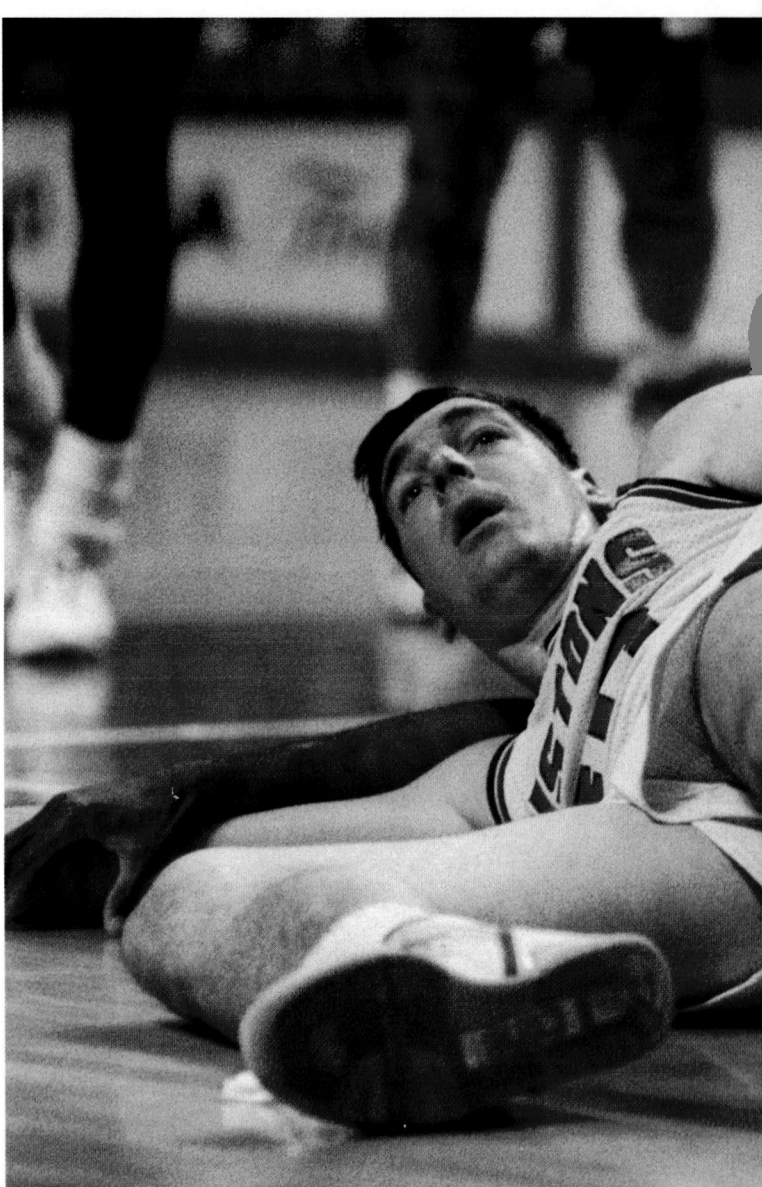

Although Joe Dumars sometimes found his path blocked by the likes of Terry Porter, there was no denying him 20 points. Nor was Bill Laimbeer one to take the Blazers lying down. He heard the wake-up call and contributed 11 points and 15 rebounds.

taken away. You could hear the crowd rumbling: "What's he doing? Tell him to pass it more."

But on nights like this, Thomas is the quickest flint the Pistons have. As go-to players go, he's a good choice, especially when he's driving and hitting from outside. So he went down the lane and scooped it in, and went down the lane and hung for a bank shot, and pulled up outside and let the ball fly, his arms straight out, his wrists bent in textbook form. You can argue with his decisions. On this night, you couldn't argue with the results. "He's our captain; he does things like that," Daly said. "That was one of his great performances."

What about that ammonia capsule?

"Old high school trick," Daly said. "Goes back to Punxsutawney High in Pennsylvania. Hey, we needed something. I'm just glad we had a few of those in the bag."

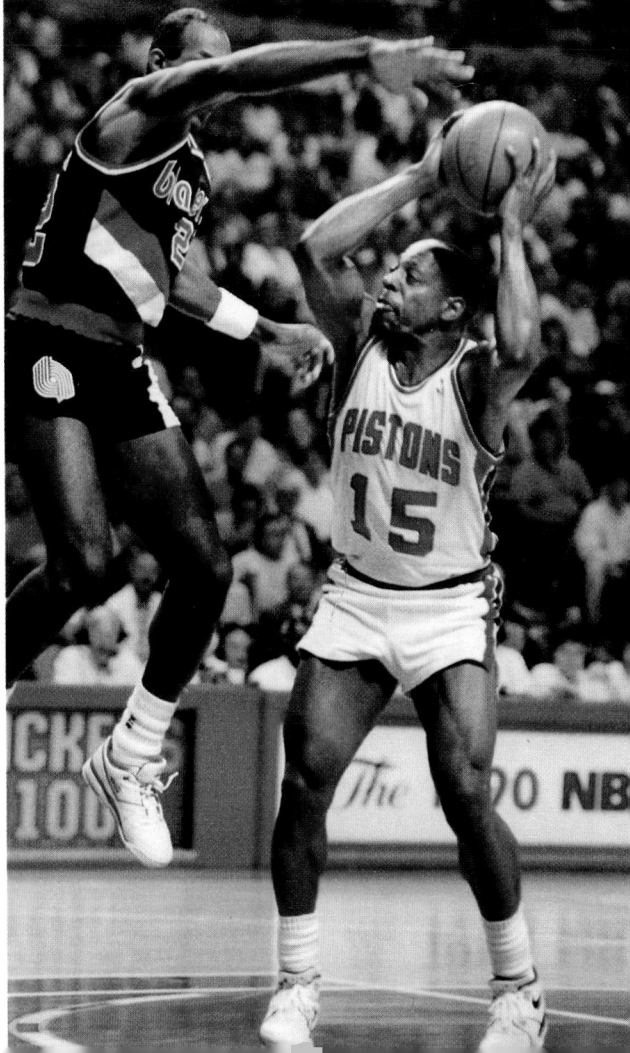

Wake up and smell the victory.

Or, in Portland's case, the defeat. The Blazers had the champions down at home. They let them up. They failed to score for more than four minutes down the stretch.

"Detroit shut us down late in the game," Williams said. That's being polite. The Blazers were rattled in those final minutes. They took bad shots, made bad decisions and did not rebound. They were overwhelmed.

The Pistons were fortunate to win. They finished the game with 37 percent shooting. But you win any way you can, even if it's with your smallest player on the floor. And even if he got a little help from an ammonia tablet.

"Those things are like getting punched in the nose," Thomas said, making a face. "You know how your eyes get all full of water. . . . ?"

We knew. And so did Portland. ∎

Portland's defense kept the Microwave on low. Vinnie Johnson finished with two points.

PORTLAND: GAME 2

By Mitch Albom

This time, there was no magic. No Isiah, either. This time it was the Portland Trail Blazers who proved that what counts is not how you start but how you finish, and this is how they finished: on top. "Take that!" the Blazers seemed to say as they raced off the Palace court June 7, ending a heart-thumping overtime marathon, 106-105, to tie the NBA Finals at one game apiece. "Take that, Detroit! You might know fourth quarters, but we know what to do in overtime."

Yeah. You know what they did? They hit their free throws. They got enough of them. The Blazers went to the line 41 times and the Pistons went 23, and anyone who says you get the calls at home can have this game tattooed to his forehead. The most common picture of the night was Chuck Daly, dropping his head in front of the bench as the echo of the whistle rattled in his ears. He stood in that pose with two seconds left in the overtime, when Portland's Clyde Drexler stuck in the dagger, dropping two free throws and putting an end to what could have been one of the most dramatic stories in Pistons playoff history. Drama? Did we say drama? How about Bill Laimbeer going nuts from three-point range, hitting six for the night — tying a finals record — including one rainbow that should have won this thing in the final seconds. It put the Pistons on top, 105-104. How about Dennis Rodman, the best defensive player in the league, getting called for a questionable foul on Drexler, then falling to his knees in disbelief. How about James Edwards, who pulled every kind of shot out of his weathered bag — he made most of them — and here he was going up for the final attempt of the night, milliseconds left, taking two Portland bodies with him, getting no call, and seeing the ball clank off the side of the backboard.

"AW, COME ON! COME ON!" screamed Chuck Daly. The refs just stared at him. The crowd went silent. Sometimes the end is not the best part. "After I hit that shot," Laimbeer said, "I looked at the clock and saw four seconds, which is an eternity in the NBA." He was right.

But what should concern the Pistons more than the final seconds was the big chunk of

basketball in the middle. Does anyone remember the second and third quarters, when this game was probably lost? Attention all units: Be on the lookout for a missing Pistons offense. That's the real problem. There will be much talk about the officials and some will be justified. But when your blood stops boiling and you cleanse the memory of Isiah Thomas missing the final shot in regulation and fouling out in overtime, this, if you look carefully, is what you will see: The Pistons should not have been in that situation to begin with. They were at home, they had every reason to be confident, and yet for the middle quarters they played like a college freshman slumped over his

Vice President Dan Quayle and son Tucker saw James Edwards rise up for 26 points, but the Buddha's final shot, after he had beaten Wayne Cooper, was partially deflected by Cliff Robinson.

typewriter, head in hands, trying to come up with an opening paragraph.

This is an offense? Thomas, bouncing at the top of the key, waiting, waiting, then finally spinning in and forcing something. Mark Aguirre, standing at the top of the key, passing up an open shot, then after eight seconds of nothing, taking that same shot — only now with a defender in his face. What happened to Joe Dumars' contribution in this thing? Wasn't he the Pistons' leading scorer this season? What happened to the pass? What on Earth is wrong with Vinnie Johnson? He has made one basket in this series, and it was a lay-up. Yes, Portland is playing good defense on

Detroit's favorite plays — dumping it in to Edwards or running a screen for Dumars — but the Pistons are a bright enough bunch to come up with counters for that, aren't they? Haven't other teams known their favorite plays all year?

This unimaginative offense has forced the defense to be miraculous, and while it often lives up to the billing, it can't do it every night. There's something more at work. Something inside. "It's hard to understand," Daly said. "We've come all this way and suddenly we lose our emotion for winning? Maybe it's too many games in too many years. It may be fatigue. Whatever. I don't see the emotion in wanting to win the way we once had it." Whoa. If that doesn't scare you, nothing will.

"We have the home-court advantage," Blazers coach Rick Adelman boasted. Well. A word about that. For all the noise about what a huge difference the home court makes, remember that in 1988 and 1989, the visiting team won Game 3 in the finals. Sure, the Pistons haven't won in Portland in 16 years. But those 20 losses were often a year apart. These next three will be two days' apart. If you don't know the difference, you don't understand sports. "We got to go to Portland," Laimbeer said, "take our raincoats and win some games." ∎

Dennis Rodman, despite a sore ankle, held Jerome Kersey to six points. But Rodman scored only one point and committed a crucial late foul. "All I'm doing," he said, "is taking up space. I feel I'm letting the team down."

GAME 2 BOX

Trail Blazers 106, Pistons 105 (OT)

Thursday, June 7, 1990, at Auburn Hills, Mich.

PORTLAND	MIN	FG	3PT	FT	REB	AST	PF	PTS
Jerome Kersey	38	3-11	0-0	0-0	0-3	0	6	6
Buck Williams	46	3-9	0-0	6-8	4-12	1	2	12
Kevin Duckworth	28	6-10	0-0	2-3	1-8	0	6	14
Clyde Drexler	43	13-20	1-2	6-8	0-3	3	3	33
Terry Porter	42	3-11	0-4	15-15	1-4	10	0	21
Wayne Cooper	21	1-4	0-0	1-2	2-5	0	5	3
Danny Young	11	1-3	0-0	0-0	0-1	1	2	2
Cliff Robinson	21	2-8	0-0	3-5	0-1	2	0	7
Drazen Petrovic	13	4-5	0-0	0-0	0-0	0	2	8
Mark Bryant	2	0-0	0-0	0-0	1-1	0	0	0
TOTALS	265	36-81	1-6	33-41	9-38	17	26	106

Percentages: FG .444, 3PT .167, FT .805. Team rebounds: 15. Blocked shots: 3 (Robinson 2, Kersey). Turnovers: 11 (Drexler 4, Duckworth 3, Williams 3, Porter). Steals: 9 (Porter 3, Drexler 2, Cooper, Petrovic, Robinson, Williams). Illegal defense: 3. Technicals: Illegal defense 2, 4:46 second, 11:36 third.

DETROIT	MIN	FG	3PT	FT	REB	AST	PF	PTS
Dennis Rodman	25	0-1	0-0	1-2	2-8	1	4	1
James Edwards	38	12-23	0-0	2-3	2-4	0	5	26
Bill Laimbeer	44	10-18	6-9	0-0	4-11	4	4	26
Joe Dumars	46	6-11	0-0	4-5	1-6	8	3	16
Isiah Thomas	44	9-21	2-4	3-6	3-7	11	6	23
John Salley	32	1-3	0-0	3-5	2-6	0	1	5
Vinnie Johnson	16	1-4	0-0	0-0	1-1	0	3	2
Mark Aguirre	20	2-9	0-1	2-2	0-1	1	2	6
TOTALS	265	41-90	8-14	15-23	15-44	25	28	105

Percentages: FG .456, 3PT .571, FT .652. Team rebounds: 13. Blocked shots: 7 (Salley 3, Thomas 2, Edwards, Johnson). Turnovers: 18 (Thomas 7, Dumars 3, Aguirre 2, Johnson 2, Rodman 2, Edwards, Salley). Steals: 2 (Laimbeer, Thomas). Technicals: Suhr, 6:52 second.

PORTLAND	23	30	22	19	12—106
DETROIT	30	15	24	25	11—105

Attendance: 21,454. Time: 3:14. Officials: Darell Garretson, Jack Madden, Hue Hollins.

PORTLAND: GAME 3

By Mitch Albom

He had been braced for this death for weeks, calling the hospital, hoping against hope, even instructing his wife, Debbie, "If Dad dies during a game, I want you to promise me you'll be the one to tell me, OK? And not until after the game is over. Just you, OK?"

She promised. Now the game was over. Sweat was pouring off his arms and face. Joe Dumars took a last look at the scoreboard and walked off the court, happy the Pistons were back in this championship hunt. He could hardly wait to call home and tell them — and then his coach, Chuck Daly, pulled him aside. His wife was on the phone.

This is a story about courage and effort and life and death — and perspective. Yes, Joe's dad was always big on perspective. He had no legs, no mobility, but he had a heart as big as Louisiana,

Bill Laimbeer and Mark Aguirre could enjoy the game's closing moments because Vinnie Johnson ended a 3-for-25 shooting slump with 21 points.

where he lived, and he passed it on to his son, and his son has been passing it on to Detroiters every day he pulls on a uniform. Once, early in his career, Dumars called home after a game and his father got on the phone. "I saw you today on the TV, son. You played good. And they pay you for that?" "Yeah, dad," Joe said, laughing, "they do." "That's a good job you got there. Hang on to it." "OK, Dad. I will."

It was that kind of love, one of those quiet relationships in which you go right from childhood to adulthood and you never stop thinking your dad is the smartest man on earth. Joe Dumars thought that. Every day of his life. He thought it Sunday morning, June 10, before he went out and showed the country how great a basketball player he is, and no doubt he was thinking it Sunday night, as he sat in his hotel room, his mind a million miles from the NBA Finals.

"This hurts so much because we all know how tight they were," said forward John Salley, shaking his head, after Detroit's 121-106 victory in Game 3, which went from very important to not important at all. The players had been slapping each others' backs, proud of the spirit they had shown in Portland's raucous, foreign arena, and suddenly the word spread and the room went quiet and nobody was slapping each other anymore. Could there be a more poignant afternoon? Can fate really be this . . . ironic? Here was Dumars, playing the hottest game of the NBA Finals, scoring 33 points, leading the Pistons from the depths of their own despair to a victory that put them right back on the track for a championship. He was making shots from the ground and from midair and from ridiculous angles — he was amazing — and all afternoon, the whole time, he never knew. His father. Joe Dumars II, 65, had died just hours before the game, from congestive heart failure. The Pistons had gotten the phone call; Daly, the assistant coaches and captain Isiah Thomas had been informed. No one else. And not Joe. They kept Debbie's promise. They said nothing.

Now here was Thomas running the floor with his teammate, trying not to look at him too often, as if his face might give it away. How tough was this? "I knew something that would shatter his world," Thomas said, shaking his head. He sat in the office when Dumars got the phone call. Then Dumars was gone, whisked away so he would not have to deal with reporters prying into his private tragedy. Thomas got up and carried his teammate's No. 4 jersey, still soaked with the afternoon's sweat. He folded it neatly and walked down the corridor. "It really puts everything in perspective," Thomas said.

Perspective. It was no surprise that in June 1989, when the Pistons realized their dream of the NBA title, when the champagne was poured over their heads and they were dancing and singing, Dumars told a reporter that "this ring goes to my dad." The greatest thing he had accomplished should, naturally, go to the greatest man he knew, right?

Perspective. Suddenly, the whole championship was cast in a sad light, this whole crazy series that had people so up in arms about who had the better city and who got the bad foul calls and who pushed off when he shot —

Guards Joe Dumars, Isiah Thomas and Vinnie Johnson combined for 75 points and 60.5 percent shooting (26-for-43). After talking with his mother, Ophelia, Dumars decided to stay in Portland until his father's funeral, six days after his death.

suddenly all that was very small, and it could never be that big again. Dumars would return soon to the house where his father constructed his first basketball hoop — a sawed-off door and a bicycle rim — and you can bet he wouldn't think about his 33 points or another championship.

The other Pistons were noticeably upset by the death. Vinnie Johnson, who had his best game of the playoffs, who snapped out of his slump for 21 points, who should have wanted to be interviewed more than anyone else, stood before an army of reporters and said, "I don't want to talk now, OK?" Brendan Suhr, who lost his father to the same killing disease the previous summer, stood out on the court, wiping tears from his eyes. "We talked about the disease a lot; we compared stories," Suhr said. "I told him how much it hurt when my father died, but how you draw strength from it in the end."

In the end, that is the best any of us can hope for Dumars. That he draws comfort and strength.

"There was this one shot today," Thomas said, allowing a small smile, "where Joe came down the lane, and he threw it up, real high, and it went way up and fell through. I looked at him and I said to myself, 'Your father put that one in, Joe.'"

Amen. ∎

GAME 3 BOX

Pistons 121, Trail Blazers 106

Sunday, June 10, 1990, at Portland, Ore.

DETROIT	MIN	FG	3PT	FT	REB	AST	PF	PTS
Mark Aguirre	28	4-7	1-2	2-4	1-3	1	2	11
James Edwards	25	5-10	0-0	1-5	1-2	2	2	11
Bill Laimbeer	40	4-12	0-3	3-3	1-12	2	6	11
Joe Dumars	43	11-22	2-3	9-9	1-1	5	3	33
Isiah Thomas	41	6-8	0-1	9-11	1-5	8	4	21
John Salley	21	3-7	0-0	4-4	3-7	1	3	10
David Greenwood	13	1-1	0-0	1-2	1-5	0	4	3
Scott Hastings	3	0-1	0-1	0-0	0-0	0	1	0
Vinnie Johnson	25	9-13	0-0	3-3	1-1	0	1	21
Gerald Henderson	1	0-0	0-0	0-0	0-0	0	0	0
TOTALS	240	43-81	3-10	32-41	10-36	19	26	121

Percentages: FG .531, 3PT .300, FT .780. Team rebounds: 13. Blocked shots: 4 (Salley 2, Laimbeer, Johnson). Turnovers: 14 (Thomas 6, Dumars 4, Johnson 3, Greenwood). Steals: 3 (Aguirre, Laimbeer, Thomas). Technical fouls: Daly, 9:16 second; Edwards, 9:17 third; Laimbeer, 7:20 third.

PORTLAND	MIN	FG	3PT	FT	REB	AST	PF	PTS
Jerome Kersey	38	10-21	0-0	7-7	3-7	0	5	27
Buck Williams	27	1-3	0-0	3-4	3-6	1	6	5
Kevin Duckworth	27	8-13	0-0	2-2	2-4	0	5	18
Clyde Drexler	43	9-23	1-6	5-6	6-13	8	4	24
Terry Porter	42	6-13	1-4	7-7	2-3	9	4	20
Cliff Robinson	14	1-7	0-1	0-0	0-1	1	5	2
Mark Bryant	7	0-0	0-0	1-2	0-1	0	3	1
Wayne Cooper	16	2-3	0-0	0-0	2-5	0	1	4
Danny Young	18	2-5	0-1	1-3	0-2	1	2	5
Drazen Petrovic	8	0-5	0-1	0-0	0-0	2	3	0
TOTALS	240	39-93	2-13	26-31	18-42	22	38	106

Percentages: FG .419, 3PT .154, FT .839. Team rebounds: 15. Blocked shots: 1 (Drexler). Turnovers: 20 (Drexler 5, Duckworth 5, Porter 4, Williams 2, Bryant, Cooper, Kersey, Petrovic). Steals: 7 (Drexler 3, Porter 2, Robinson, Young). Technical fouls: Adelman, 10:22 third; Kersey, 7:20 third. Illegal defense: 1.

DETROIT	31	27	32	31—121
PORTLAND	27	24	31	24—106

Attendance: 12,884. Time: 2:32. Officials: Jake O'Donnell, Joe Crawford, Jess Kersey.

PORTLAND: GAME 4

By Mitch Albom

They were mobbed together at the center of the court, like some riot scene at a foreign embassy, raising their hands, waving their hands away, screaming until their eyes nearly popped from their sockets.

"IT WAS GOOD! IT WAS GOOD!" insisted the Portland players.

"NO GOOD! NO GOOD!" answered Detroit.

It was bedlam, madness, the culmination of an evening that threatened to explode, so crazy was this Portland arena, so wild were the fans, so great was the prize. In the balance hung, in many ways, the NBA championship. Now the referees needed a decision.

"GOOD! GOOD!" screamed Portland.

"NO GOOD! NO GOOD!" answered Detroit.

What had happened? What crazy turn of events had led to this dispute? With the Pistons leading by one point, the Trail Blazers tried to smother them with a life-sucking press. Suddenly the pass came free to Detroit's Gerald Henderson, he was wide open, nothing but shiny hardwood court in front of him, and all he had to do was run out the clock and the Pistons were one game from another NBA title and — whoa, what's this? Henderson was dropping the ball in for a lay-up! A lay-up? And a Portland player grabbed it out of bounds, heaved a pass to Danny Young, who took a few dribbles, fired up a desperation three-point attempt — how there was time for all this is an argument we will address momentarily — and lookie here. Swish.

"GOOD! GOOD!"

"NO GOOD! NO GOOD!"

The referees huddled at center court. Earl Strom threw his arms around Mike Mathis and Hugh Evans. Pistons fans back home hollered at their TV sets. Portland fans were on their feet, stomping, screaming. Chuck Daly, who has never seen a glass that wasn't half empty or completely cracked, said to himself, "We're going to overtime." Good? No good? Good? No good.

No good it was. Which means great, as far as the Pistons were concerned. "Me? I was saying a lot of prayers," admitted John Salley after the Pistons danced off the court following that crazy

Isiah Thomas made four three-pointers in the third; Portland was 0-for-5 for the game. A sixth attempt, by Danny Young, went in — an instant too late.

exclamation point of an ending — finally, legitimately, with a 112-109 victory June 12 and an almost insurmountable 3-1 lead in the NBA Finals. "Then I looked over at Gerald and said, 'Man, you're too old to make that kind of mistake. You're 39 aren't you? Ha ha.' "

Well. He might have felt like it afterward. Yes, Henderson never should have taken that lay-up, but as he said, "I hadn't touched the ball all night and I just wanted to make sure I didn't lose it out

of bounds or something." Forgive him. He was trying to do his job. Which is more than you can say for the timekeeper. What does RIP city stand for? Rest In Peace? If the guy running the clock wasn't dead, he had no excuse. How on Earth does a player have time in 1.8 seconds — which is what the clock read after Henderson's shot — to get a pass, dribble a few times and then get off a shot? And this was Danny Young, remember, not that guy from the Federal Express commercial. "That's the biggest basket I almost made," Young said. The replays clearly showed there was no time on the clock when Young went to shoot, but the buzzer had yet to sound. Home-court advantage? OK. We're supposed to be in the same time zone, right? Ahhh. Forget it. And forget a

ridiculous sixth foul on Bill Laimbeer's sneaker — yes, he was called for tripping Clyde Drexler when all he did was go for a loose ball, which in the final minute of an NBA Finals game is something that should be allowed. And forget Portland's full-court press, which, for several desperate minutes in the fourth quarter, strangled Detroit and turned a comfortable 16-point into panic time. Forget all that. The Pistons have.

In fact, all that's left on their minds is this: Unless they completely collapse, drive to the wrong arena, take a sudden trip to Burma or develop the world's worst case of chicken pox, they are about to make history, back-to-back NBA champions, and after this night, let no one say they don't deserve it.

Here, on an evening when the Pistons had to fight injury (Dennis Rodman), tragedy (Joe Dumars) and a Portland crowd that was rabid and desperate for a victory, these 12 players showed

After the Blazers accused Bill Laimbeer of flopping to draw fouls, the fans went on the attack. He eventually fouled out of Game 6 but had 12 points and 12 rebounds.

that it's not the size of the dog in the fight, but the fight in the dog that matters. So it was that the smallest men on the team — Isiah Thomas, Joe Dumars, Vinnie Johnson — stood the tallest when the final whistle sounded.

Here was Johnson, proving that "slump" is a faddish word, lighting up the nets for 20 points, leading a charge when Thomas was saddled with foul trouble. Here was Thomas, going nuclear in the third quarter, shooting from seemingly every spot on the hardwood, dropping 22 points in those 12 minutes — he finished with 32 — and shooting as if it were after midnight in his basement court. And here was Dumars, playing despite the death of his father, his heart as heavy as any five defenders, and yet he did what he had to do, he followed what his father had always preached: Do your job, do it well, do it proud. So it was that Dumars scorched the nets for 26 points and helped make a critical steal in the final eight seconds. "Joe," said Salley, summing it up for everybody, "has the biggest heart I've ever seen." And as a result of all this, the Pistons are on the giddy lip of glory. Check your history books. No team has come back from a 3-1 deficit.

Good? No good.

Which means great for the Pistons.

Get the confetti ready. ∎

GAME 4 BOX
Pistons 112, Trail Blazers 109
Tuesday, June 12, 1990, at Portland, Ore.

DETROIT	MIN	FG	3PT	FT	REB	AST	PF	PTS
Mark Aguirre	26	1-7	1-2	0-0	1-2	2	3	3
James Edwards	19	5-10	0-0	3-4	2-7	2	5	13
Bill Laimbeer	37	4-10	2-7	2-2	3-12	3	6	12
Joe Dumars	43	9-21	0-2	8-8	0-2	4	0	26
Isiah Thomas	34	11-20	4-5	6-6	1-4	5	3	32
John Salley	31	2-8	0-0	0-0	1-4	0	6	4
Vinnie Johnson	31	9-12	0-0	2-4	3-4	3	4	20
David Greenwood	16	0-2	0-0	0-0	1-4	0	3	0
Scott Hastings	1	0-0	0-0	0-0	0-0	0	0	0
Dennis Rodman	1	0-0	0-0	0-0	0-0	0	0	0
Gerald Henderson	1	1-1	0-0	0-0	0-0	0	0	2
TOTALS	240	42-91	7-16	21-24	12-39	19	30	112

Percentages: FG .462, 3PT .438, FT .875. Team rebounds: 10. Blocked shots: 3 (Salley 2, Laimbeer). Turnovers: 12 (Dumars 3, Thomas 3, Aguirre, Edwards, Greenwood, Johnson, Laimbeer, Salley). Steals: 8 (Thomas 3, Laimbeer 2, Aguirre, Dumars, Greenwood).

PORTLAND	MIN	FG	3PT	FT	REB	AST	PF	PTS
Jerome Kersey	44	11-17	0-0	11-14	1-8	2	3	33
Buck Williams	45	3-8	0-0	3-4	1-7	2	2	9
Kevin Duckworth	21	3-7	0-0	2-2	0-3	0	4	8
Clyde Drexler	41	14-19	0-1	6-9	3-8	10	2	34
Terry Porter	42	5-10	0-3	7-9	0-5	6	5	17
Wayne Cooper	12	0-1	0-0	0-0	2-2	1	2	0
Danny Young	17	0-2	0-1	0-0	0-1	1	3	0
Drazen Petrovic	4	0-1	0-0	0-0	0-1	0	1	0
Cliff Robinson	14	4-8	0-0	0-1	1-1	0	3	8
TOTALS	240	40-73	0-5	29-39	8-36	22	25	109

Percentages: FG .548, 3PT .000, FT .744. Team rebounds: 10. Blocked shots: 5 (Cooper 2, Duckworth, Kersey, Robinson). Turnovers: 18 (Porter 5, Kersey 4, Drexler 3, Duckworth 3, Cooper, Petrovic, Robinson). Steals: 5 (Kersey 2, Drexler 2, Robinson). Illegal defense: 1.

DETROIT	22	29	32	29—112
PORTLAND	32	14	27	36—109

Attendance: 12,642. Time: 2:43. Officials: Earl Strom, Mike Mathis, Hugh Evans.

PORTLAND: GAME 5

By Mitch Albom

The shot went up, the shot swished through, and suddenly the Pistons were dancing off the court and into the castle on the clouds, carrying the scars and lumps and exhausted smiles that told you the journey was tough, the journey was costly, but the journey, finally, was over.

Twice is nice.

Vinnie Johnson took the title-winning shot over the objections of Portland's Jerome Kersey. "I never made a shot like that before," Johnson said. "I used to do it all the time in college, but this was the first time I did it in the pros." Earlier in Game 5, James Edwards hooked the Blazers for 13 points.

"BACK TO BACK, BABY!" they sang in their champagne locker room, dancing and wiggling back to back, after beating the Trail Blazers, 92-90, June 14 at Memorial Coliseum. The Pistons won with a last-minute flourish — and a last-second jump shot by Vinnie Johnson — to capture their second straight NBA championship. "We won! BACK TO BACK, BABY!" Back to back, indeed. Back to glory. Back-to-back crowns on their heads, something only two other franchises — the Celtics and Lakers — have accomplished in NBA history. They did it with stamina, perseverance, desire, and, ho-ho, just a little drama. You weren't scared when they trailed by seven points with two minutes to go in a foreign arena, were you? Hey. This team thrives on that stuff.

So it was that Johnson got that look in his eye and locked his radar on the basket, jumper, jumper, nothing but net. And Bill Laimbeer got that tight jaw, and rose above the Portland players and grabbed rebound after rebound, his 16th, his 17th. And Isiah Thomas threw a prayer into the air and the prayer was answered. Good! Tie game! The crowd was swallowing its tongue. The Pistons' bench was hollering encouragement. John Salley hid his head in a towel — "I couldn't watch" — and coach Chuck Daly felt his stomach flip over. The clock ticked down — ". . . four, three, two . . ." — and finally, Johnson, one of the guys who can remember when this team couldn't give away a ticket, left the ground and let it fly and you knew it was over. They knew it in Portland, and they knew it in the sold-out Palace in Auburn Hills, Mich., where 21,500 were watching on giant TV screens.

Swish! Twice is nice.

"Vinnie said, 'Gimme the rock,'" Salley recalled, wiping champagne from his eyes. "And we said, 'Oh, you want it? OK.'" Johnson credited Laimbeer: "I was kind of down on myself in the first half, and Bill kept me in the game. He said the second half was going to be my half, and he told me I would hit the big shot down the stretch. No kidding, he did." Johnson laughed and doused himself again. "It's the biggest shot of my life!"

Go ahead. Splash Vinnie. Splash Buddha. Splash Zeke. Splash Chuck. Splash them all. But know this: It was damn tough to get there. These were not the smooth young colts who galloped to the title in 1989 without missing a beat. These were tired warriors, wearing the strain of all

those nights during the endless season when the opposing team wanted a piece of the champions. These Pistons were hobbled. They were cut, bleeding. Dennis Rodman was rolling on a bum ankle. Isiah Thomas was swallowing blood from a blow to the nose. James Edwards was taped above the eye. Joe Dumars was playing with the memory of his father, who passed away June 10, still tugging at his insides.

But here was the heart of a champion shining through. The last nine points of the game? On a foreign court? What do you call that?

Call it another championship. Twice is nice.

"Was this sweeter than last time?" someone asked Thomas, who scored 29 points and was easily voted NBA Finals most valuable player. "It was, because people doubted we could do it this time," he said, tugging on a new cap that read, "Back to back NBA champions." "We're not as physically talented as last year. But we're smarter." And they're in the record books. Remember, not only did they win successive NBA titles, but in doing so they lost *just one game in the finals*, and — almost incredibly — did not drop *a single finals game on the road*. It takes a full team to do that. How fitting then, that they were all

Finals MVP Isiah Thomas drove the Blazers to distraction with a game-high 29 points. In the Palace, 21,500 fans — some paying scalpers $30 for $3 tickets — watched on scoreboard TV. In the Pistons' locker room, a champagne shampoo rewarded Bill Laimbeer.

dancing back to back, all these players, subs and starters, relieved, overjoyed, exhausted. And how fitting that each of them had at least one moment in this post-season run, even from the farthest end of the bench. William Bedford? He was in there against Chicago. Gerald Henderson? He scored maybe the weirdest basket — the almost disastrous lay-up to end Game 4.

David Greenwood and Scott Hastings? Here were two veterans who had turned to eating popcorn during regular-season games, so useless did they feel. And yet against Portland, suddenly they were out there together — not in garbage time, mind you, but in crucial junctures.

As for the others, well, call them the Starting Eight, for at any given moment, any one was the star. How many games did Detroit win thanks to James (Buddha) Edwards — "We're riding the Buddha Train!" they used to sing in the locker room — and how many nights did Mark Aguirre pull their bacon from the fire with a sudden explosion of indoor and outdoor shooting?

Johnson? Critics buried him after Game 2 — "too old, he's done" — and yet out came the Microwave to scorch the Blazers in Games 3, 4 and 5. Amazing. And what about John Salley, the only team member to do a nightclub comedy routine. Wasn't it delightful to see him get serious once the whistle blew, rising on his jets, blocking Patrick Ewing, blocking Michael Jordan, blocking

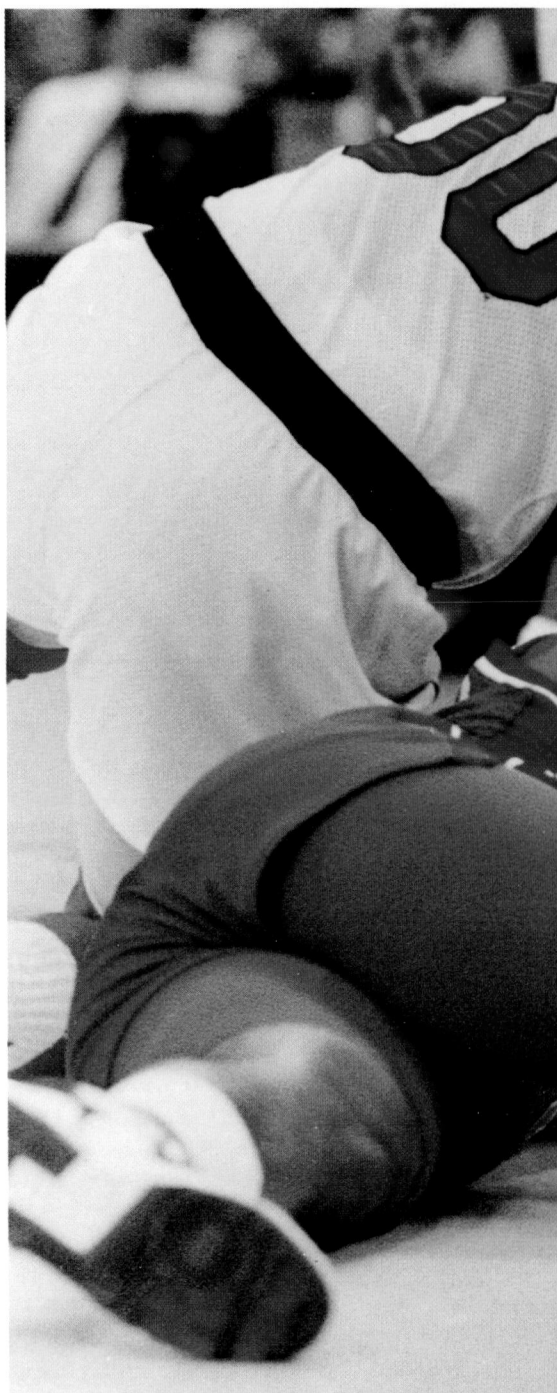

In some places, celebration of the Pistons' victory turned to mayhem and tragedy, leaving at least eight dead and scores injured. Friends of one victim, a 15-year-old girl, tied flowers and a photo to a light pole on Van Dyke in Detroit, near where she was killed by a hit-and-run driver.

Clyde Drexler. The Joker is growing up, folks.

Laimbeer? He deserves some kind of award, maybe the Joyce Brothers Award, for crawling into the Blazers' heads and screwing them up. He kneaded them, nudged them, outrebounded them, outglared them. By the end, they were so irritated by his presence, they were like a man destroying his house trying to kill a fly. And after each victory, Laimbeer, who still can't run or jump worth a nickel, smirked and said, "Whatever it takes." Weren't you glad he was on Detroit's side? And wouldn't you say that about Rodman, awaited will forever be etched in his memory. "It was awful hard," he finally admitted. "Sometimes I was dying out there." But he wasn't alone. "When my shot went in," Johnson said, "I grabbed Joe and said that was for our dads. My father passed away in October. Now we're here and . . . I just told Joe, this is for our pops, man."

What can you say after that? Nothing. Just as there was nothing for the Trail Blazers to say. They gave a good effort, but they crumbled at the end, as inexperienced teams do. Even the normally crazed Portland fans seemed to sense it. Finally, they could only stand and applaud the Detroit conquerors as they ran off the court. Nice. And why not, when you consider this list: Boston, Milwaukee, Chicago, Los Angeles Lakers, Indiana, New York, Chicago and Portland. The Pistons chopped them all down over two post-seasons. That's serious stuff.

In the end, it's the team scenes that stay with you: Salley palming Thomas' head and rubbing it joyously. Rodman hurling himself into the arms of a startled Aguirre. Hastings and Greenwood kissing each other for the cameras. And finally, all of them, dousing each other with champagne and wiggling in unbridled joy for all they've done, all they've endured, all they've accomplished. "BACK TO BACK, BABY!"

Twice is nice. Anybody for three? ■

that long walk to the office where the phone call who drove himself to tears battling his own bones, fighting to play on that bum ankle, jumping on a trampoline during games to stay warm? And for all Rodman was unable to do, Thomas seemed doubly capable. His shooting seemed to come from the gods — they kissed each ball in mid-air and, swish, it fell through.

Thomas' magnificence was matched only by the courage of his backcourt mate, Dumars, who will never forget the finals; he can't. His father died just hours before his best game, Game 3, and

Try as he might, 270-pound Kevin Duckworth couldn't keep Mark Aguirre and Detroit down. Champagne-soaked Chuck Daly chatted with CBS' Pat O'Brien.

With John Salley coming on strong and Isiah Thomas leading in style, the Pistons were destined to double their NBA title holdings.

GAME 5 BOX

Pistons 92, Trail Blazers 90

Thursday, June 14, 1990, at Portland, Ore.

DETROIT	MIN	FG	3PT	FT	REB	AST	PF	PTS
Mark Aguirre	18	3-8	1-1	3-3	2-4	0	3	10
James Edwards	34	5-13	0-0	3-5	1-3	0	5	13
Bill Laimbeer	33	3-5	0-1	0-0	1-17	2	5	6
Joe Dumars	37	2-13	0-1	4-6	3-4	7	2	8
Isiah Thomas	35	13-20	3-3	0-2	2-3	5	3	29
John Salley	25	4-8	0-0	0-0	4-6	0	4	8
Dennis Rodman	30	1-3	0-0	0-2	2-5	1	3	2
Vinnie Johnson	24	6-11	0-0	4-5	1-2	0	3	16
David Greenwood	4	0-0	0-0	0-0	0-0	0	1	0
TOTALS	**240**	**37-81**	**4-6**	**14-23**	**16-44**	**15**	**29**	**92**

Percentages: FG .457, 3PT .667, FT .609. Team rebounds: 10. Blocked shots: 6 (Rodman 2, Edwards, Johnson, Laimbeer, Salley). Turnovers: 18 (Thomas 7, Edwards 3, Aguirre 2, Dumars 2, Johnson 2, Rodman, Salley). Steals: 9 (Dumars 2, Thomas 2, Edwards, Johnson, Laimbeer, Rodman, Salley). Illegal defense: 1. Technical fouls: Laimbeer, 2:41 third.

PORTLAND	MIN	FG	3PT	FT	REB	AST	PF	PTS
Jerome Kersey	45	4-12	0-1	3-4	4-9	3	4	11
Buck Williams	33	5-11	0-0	0-0	2-8	2	4	10
Kevin Duckworth	37	10-21	0-0	1-3	0-5	0	3	21
Clyde Drexler	40	6-13	0-1	8-11	1-6	4	6	20
Terry Porter	40	5-12	4-9	7-10	1-1	9	2	21
Wayne Cooper	11	1-3	0-0	0-2	1-3	0	2	2
Danny Young	16	2-2	1-1	0-0	1-2	2	1	5
Cliff Robinson	18	0-4	0-0	0-0	4-6	0	3	0
TOTALS	**240**	**33-78**	**5-12**	**19-30**	**14-40**	**20**	**25**	**90**

Percentages: FG .423, 3PT .417, FT .633. Team rebounds: 15. Blocked shots: 4 (Porter, Robinson, Williams, Young). Turnovers: 17 (Porter 5, Drexler 4, Kersey 3, Robinson 2, Williams 2, Duckworth). Steals: 8 (Porter 3, Cooper, Drexler, Duckworth, Kersey, Young). Technical fouls: Kersey, 2:41 third. Fouled out: Drexler.

DETROIT				
	26	20	19	27—92

PORTLAND				
	22	20	27	21—90

Attendance: 12,642. Time: 2:30. Officials: Darell Garretson, Ed T. Rush, Jack Madden.

COMPOSITE BOX

Pistons (4-1)

PLAYER	G	MIN	FG%	FT%	REB	AST	PTS
Isiah Thomas	5	38.4	.542	.742	5.2	7.0	27.6
Joe Dumars	5	42.0	.415	.892	2.8	5.6	20.6
James Edwards	5	27.6	.446	.560	3.8	0.8	14.4
Bill Laimbeer	5	38.2	.444	1.00	13.4	2.4	13.2
Vinnie Johnson	5	22.6	.543	.786	2.0	1.2	12.2
Mark Aguirre	5	24.0	.333	.667	3.6	0.8	9.6
John Salley	5	28.6	.375	.692	6.4	0.4	6.6
Dennis Rodman	4	19.8	.444	.250	5.5	0.8	2.3
David Greenwood	3	11.0	.333	.500	3.0	0.0	1.0
Gerald Henderson	2	1.0	1.00	.000	0.0	0.0	1.0
Scott Hastings	2	2.0	.000	.000	0.0	0.0	0.0
TOTALS	**5**	**—**	**.454**	**.739**	**43.4**	**18.8**	**107.0**

Three-point goals: Thomas 11-16 (.688), Aguirre 4-8 (.500), Laimbeer 8-23 (.348), Dumars 2-7 (.286), Hastings 0-1 (.000), Johnson 0-1 (.000). Totals: 25-56 (.446). **Team rebounds:** 65. **Blocked shots:** 25 (Salley 12, Edwards 3, Johnson 3, Laimbeer 3, Rodman 2, Thomas 2). **Turnovers:** 76 (Thomas 25, Dumars 18, Johnson 8, Aguirre 6, Rodman 6, Edwards 5, Salley 4, Greenwood 2, Laimbeer, team). **Steals:** 28 (Thomas 8, Laimbeer 7, Dumars 4, Aguirre 2, Rodman 2, Edwards 2, Greenwood, Johnson, Salley).

Trail Blazers (1-4)

PLAYER	G	MIN	FG%	FT%	REB	AST	PTS
Clyde Drexler	5	40.8	.543	.757	7.8	6.2	26.4
Jerome Kersey	5	41.2	.473	.781	7.0	1.2	19.0
Terry Porter	5	41.2	.393	.889	2.6	8.4	19.0
Kevin Duckworth	5	29.8	.523	.667	5.6	0.0	15.6
Buck Williams	5	38.4	.465	.640	9.0	1.8	11.2
Cliff Robinson	5	16.4	.250	.500	2.4	0.8	3.8
Danny Young	5	15.6	.400	.333	1.4	1.6	3.0
Drazen Petrovic	4	7.3	.357	.000	0.3	0.5	2.5
Wayne Cooper	5	14.0	.333	.250	4.0	0.2	1.8
Mark Bryant	2	4.5	.000	.500	1.0	0.0	0.5
TOTALS	**5**	**—**	**.456**	**.740**	**40.4**	**20.6**	**102.0**

Three-point goals: Young 2-6 (.333), Porter 7-25 (.280), Drexler 2-12 (.167), Petrovic 0-1 (.000), Robinson 0-1 (.000), Kersey 0-2 (.000). Totals: 11-47 (.234). **Team rebounds:** 61. **Blocked shots:** 17 (Cooper 4, Robinson 4, Kersey 3, Duckworth 2, Drexler, Porter, Williams, Young). **Turnovers:** 83 (Porter 22, Drexler 17, Duckworth 15, Kersey 8, Williams 8, Young 4, Petrovic 3, Robinson 2, Cooper 2, Bryant, team). **Steals:** 36 (Porter 10, Drexler 9, Robinson 4, Kersey 3, Williams 3, Young 3, Cooper 2, Duckworth, Petrovic).

DETROIT					
	133	114	136	141	11—535

PORTLAND					
	137	107	135	119	12—510

THE NUMBERS

Dennis Rodman covered plenty of ground on the court. His likeness covered plenty of faces in the stands. His numbers made him the top defensive player in the NBA.

GAME-BY-GAME

Regular season

Detroit home games in capitals

DATE	SCORE	OPPONENT	W-L	PLACE	TOP SCORER	TOP REBOUNDER	OPP. SCORER
11-3	106-103	NEW YORK	1-0	1st (tied)	Dumars (26)	Aguirre (9)	Ewing (23)
11-4	95-93	Washington	2-0	1st (tied)	Thomas (28)	Salley, Laimbeer (9)	Malone (19)
11-7	114-117	Chicago	2-1	2nd (T), ½ GB	Dumars (23)	Rodman (8)	Jordan (40)
11-8	74-95	Indiana	2-2	5th, 1½ GB	Thomas (17)	Rodman (15)	Fleming (22)
11-10	125-121	Orlando	3-2	3rd (T), 1½ GB	Thomas (29)	Laimbeer (10)	Catledge (27)
11-11	84-88	Miami	3-3	4th, 2 GB	Thomas (19)	Salley (12)	Edwards, Seikaly (21)
11-15	130-94	MIAMI	4-3	4th, 1 GB	Dumars (24)	Rodman, Salley (11)	Frank (16)
11-17	106-79	MILWAUKEE	5-3	2nd (T), .042 B	Dumars (22)	Rodman (12)	Pierce, Sikma (16)
11-18	103-86	BOSTON	6-3	1st, ½ GA	Dumars (27)	Laimbeer (12)	Bird (22)
11-21	96-103	ATLANTA	6-4	2nd, .025 B	Thomas (32)	Rodman (10)	Malone (27)
11-24	101-82	CLEVELAND	7-4	2nd, .031 B	Dumars (31)	Laimbeer (9)	Price (14)
11-26	82-102	Portland	7-5	2nd (T), ½ GB	Aguirre (22)	Laimbeer (9)	Drexler (27)
11-28	93-81	Sacramento	8-5	2nd, .021 B	Dumars (16)	Laimbeer (13)	Ainge (20)
11-29	111-103	Phoenix	9-5	2nd, .024 B	Thomas (29)	Laimbeer (13)	Chambers (25)
12-1	108-97	LA Lakers (OT)	10-5	2nd, .025 B	Dumars (26)	Rodman (14)	Johnson (28)
12-2	95-120	Seattle	10-6	2nd, ½ GB	Johnson, Rodman, Thomas (13)	Rodman (8)	Ellis (30)
12-6	115-107	WASHINGTON	11-6	2nd, ½ GB	Laimbeer (29)	Laimbeer (23)	King (25)
12-8	101-107	Philadelphia	11-7	3rd, 1½ GB	Thomas (21)	Laimbeer (9)	Dawkins (26)
12-9	121-93	INDIANA	12-7	3rd, ½ GB	Thomas (30)	Rodman (14)	Schrempf (20)
12-12	121-108	Denver	13-7	3rd, ½ GB	Aguirre (29)	Laimbeer (10)	Davis (27)
12-13	79-83	LA Clippers	13-8	4th, 1 GB	Thomas (18)	Rodman (14)	Harper, Grant, Manning, Norman (15)
12-15	91-94	Utah	13-9	4th, 1½ GB	Dumars (26)	Laimbeer (14)	Malone (27)
12-16	92-104	Golden State	13-10	4th, 2 GB	Aguirre (31)	Rodman (14)	Mullin (27)
12-19	94-77	SEATTLE	14-10	4th, 2 GB	Aguirre (21)	Laimbeer (11)	Threatt (18)
12-22	96-90	New Jersey	15-10	4th, 1½ GB	Dumars (27)	Laimbeer, Aguirre (8)	Hopson (19)
12-23	106-100	ORLANDO	16-10	4th, ½ GB	Thomas (21)	Rodman (13)	Theus (30)
12-27	99-82	Cleveland	17-10	3rd, ½ GB	Edwards (25)	Laimbeer, Rodman (12)	Price (22)
12-29	85-99	MILWAUKEE	17-11	4th, 1½ GB	Aguirre (19)	Laimbeer (9)	Roberts (20)
12-30	117-106	NEW JERSEY	18-11	3rd, 1½ GB	Dumars, Edwards (18)	Laimbeer (13)	Hinson (21)
1-2	115-113	Orlando	19-11	3rd, 1 GB	Laimbeer (26)	Rodman (8)	Smith (28)
1-3	84-80	LA CLIPPERS	20-11	2nd, 1 GB	Thomas (29)	Salley (9)	Smith (27)
1-5	122-99	INDIANA	21-11	2nd, 1 GB	Aguirre (26)	Laimbeer (12)	Schrempf (26)
1-6	117-106	NEW YORK	22-11	2nd, .010 B	Dumars (29)	Rodman (9)	Ewing (29)
1-9	100-90	CHICAGO	23-11	1st, 1 GA	Dumars (28)	Laimbeer, Rodman (8)	Pippen (17)
1-10	97-104	Boston	23-12	1st, 1 GA	Edwards (22)	Laimbeer (12)	Lewis (32)

Regular season

Detroit home games in capitals

DATE	SCORE	OPPONENT	W-L	PLACE	TOP SCORER	TOP REBOUNDER	OPP. SCORER
1-12	97-86	MINNESOTA	24-12	1st, 1 GA	Thomas (23)	Rodman (15)	Campbell (28)
1-13	111-106	PORTLAND	25-12	1st, 1 GA	Dumars (27)	Laimbeer (12)	Drexler (17)
1-17	108-112	Philadelphia	25-13	1st, 1 GA	Edwards (32)	Rodman (9)	Barkley (30)
1-19	125-118	GOLDEN ST.	26-13	1st,½ GA	Dumars (30)	Rodman (20)	Mullin (37)
1-21	97-107	LA LAKERS	26-14	2nd, ½ GB	Edwards (26)	Laimbeer (15)	Worthy (31)
1-23	107-95	Chicago	27-14	1st, ½ GA	Thomas (26)	Rodman (11)	Jordan (32)
1-26	107-103	PHOENIX	28-14	1st, 1½ GA	Laimbeer (31)	Laimbeer (23)	K. Johnson (34)
1-27	85-83	Minnesota	29-14	1st, 1½ GA	Thomas (26)	Rodman (11)	Royal (23)
1-30	112-95	Atlanta	30-14	1st, 1½ GA	Edwards (20)	Dumars, Rodman (8)	Wilkins (20)
1-31	133-109	WASHINGTON	31-14	1st, 2 GA	Aguirre (25)	Laimbeer (12)	King (23)
2-3	105-100	Cleveland	32-14	1st, 3½ GA	Dumars, Thomas (19)	Rodman (8)	Price (25)
2-4	115-83	UTAH	33-14	1st, 4 GA	Edwards (21)	Rodman (8)	Malone (19)
2-6	105-96	CLEVELAND	34-14	1st, 4½ GA	Dumars (22)	Rodman (11)	J. Williams (21)
2-8	104-101	Milwaukee	35-14	1st, 6 GA	Thomas (23)	Laimbeer (14)	Lohaus (21)

ALL-STAR GAME: Feb. 11 at Miami. Chuck Daly-coached East beats West, 130-113. MVP: Lakers guard Magic Johnson (22 points, 6 rebounds, 4 assists). Pistons: Guard Isiah Thomas (a starter), 27 minutes, 15 points, 4 rebounds, 9 assists; guard Joe Dumars, 18 minutes, 9 points, 1 rebound, 5 assists; forward Dennis Rodman, 11 minutes, 4 points, 4 rebounds, 1 assist.

DATE	SCORE	OPPONENT	W-L	PLACE	TOP SCORER	TOP REBOUNDER	OPP. SCORER
2-13	106-96	DENVER	36-14	1st, 6 GA	Thomas (17)	Laimbeer (20)	Adams (19)
2-17	97-79	Miami	37-14	1st, 6½ GA	Thomas (23)	Rodman (18)	Frank (24)
2-19	94-85	MIAMI	38-14	1st, 6 GA	Dumars (20)	Rodman (11)	Douglas (16)
2-21	140-109	ORLANDO	39-14	1st, 6½ GA	Dumars (22)	Laimbeer (12)	Wiley (20)
2-23	103-112	Atlanta	39-15	1st, 5½ GA	Thomas (23)	Salley (8)	Malone (20)
2-25	98-87	New York	40-15	1st, 5½ GA	Dumars (31)	Rodman (12)	Ewing (37)
2-27	106-102	HOUSTON (OT)	41-15	1st, 5½ GA	Thomas (37)	Edwards, Rodman (10)	Olajuwon (37)
3-1	99-85	Washington	42-15	1st, 6 GA	Thomas (24)	Rodman (15)	Malone (19)
3-2	115-112	PHILA. (OT)	43-15	1st, 6 GA	Dumars (34)	Rodman (13)	Barkley (26)
3-4	111-105	INDIANA	44-15	1st, 6 GA	Dumars, Thomas (23)	Rodman (17)	Person (29)
3-6	101-91	SACRAMENTO	45-15	1st, 6 GA	Dumars, Laimbeer (25)	Laimbeer (12)	Tisdale (40)
3-9	99-95	New Jersey	46-15	1st, 7 GA	Edwards (21)	Rodman (13)	Hopson (21)
3-11	98-88	Charlotte	47-15	1st, 7 GA	Dumars, Edwards (21)	Laimbeer (11)	Curry (21)
3-15	110-98	SAN ANTONIO	48-15	1st, 7 GA	Dumars (21)	Laimbeer, Rodman (8)	Cummings (25)
3-16	106-81	Chicago	49-15	1st, 8 GA	Edwards (21)	Rodman (8)	Jordan (20)
3-18	114-84	DALLAS	50-15	1st, 7½ GA	Edwards, Laimbeer (16)	Laimbeer (13)	Perkins (18)
3-20	117-96	Milwaukee	51-15	1st, 8 GA	Edwards (21)	Salley (13)	Pierce (21)
3-22	110-115	Houston	51-16	1st, 7 GA	Aguirre (21)	Rodman (12)	Olajuwon (26)
3-24	98-105	San Antonio	51-17	1st, 6½ GA	Aguirre (17)	Laimbeer (10)	Cummings (40)
3-25	96-98	Dallas (OT)	51-18	1st, 6 GA	Thomas (22)	Laimbeer (17)	Blackman (23)
3-28	106-97	CHARLOTTE	52-18	1st, 5½ GA	Edwards (22)	Laimbeer, Rodman (8)	Bogues, Curry (15)
3-30	111-123	Boston	52-19	1st, 4½ GA	Thomas (32)	Rodman (14)	Bird (33)
4-3	93-82	BOSTON	53-19	1st, 4 GA	Edwards (28)	Laimbeer (21)	McHale (22)

Regular season
Detroit home games in capitals

DATE	SCORE	OPPONENT	W-L	PLACE	TOP SCORER	TOP REBOUNDER	OPP. SCORER
4-5	104-99	Atlanta	54-19	1st, 4 GA	Aguirre (25)	Laimbeer (11)	Wilkins (17)
4-6	84-92	MILWAUKEE	54-20	1st, 3½ GA	Edwards (25)	Rodman (12)	Lohaus (25)
4-8	97-100	Cleveland	54-21	1st, 2½ GA	Johnson (25)	Rodman (11)	Williams (33)
4-10	108-98	New York	55-21	1st, 3 GA	Thomas (21)	Rodman (13)	Ewing (26)
4-11	98-93	NEW JERSEY	56-21	1st, 3 GA	Aguirre (22)	Laimbeer (13)	Morris, Short (19)
4-13	111-115	ATLANTA	56-22	1st, 2 GA	Edwards (29)	Johnson (8)	Wilkins (25)
4-14	111-107	ORLANDO	57-22	1st, 3 GA	Edwards (22)	Laimbeer (13)	Theus (26)
4-19	97-107	PHILADELPHIA	57-23	1st, 2 GA	Edwards (24)	Laimbeer (11)	Barkley (36)
4-20	121-115	Indiana (OT)	58-23	1st, 3 GA	Aguirre (25)	Rodman (17)	Miller (38)
4-22	111-106	CHICAGO	59-23	1st, 4 GA	Thomas (18)	Laimbeer (11)	Jordan (22)

Eastern Conference first round: Pistons vs. Pacers
Detroit home games in capitals

DATE	SCORE	OPPONENT	W-L	SERIES	TOP SCORER	TOP REBOUNDER	OPP. SCORER
4-26	104-92	INDIANA	60-23	1-0	Edwards (21)	Laimbeer (14)	Schrempf (26)
4-28	100-87	INDIANA	61-23	2-0	Laimbeer (22)	Laimbeer (11)	Miller (23)
5-1	108-96	Indiana	62-23	3-0	Thomas (23)	Laimbeer (19)	Miller (22)

Eastern Conference semifinals: Pistons vs. Knicks

DATE	SCORE	OPPONENT	W-L	SERIES	TOP SCORER	TOP REBOUNDER	OPP. SCORER
5-8	112-77	NEW YORK	63-23	1-0	Thomas (21)	Laimbeer (13)	Ewing (19)
5-10	104-97	NEW YORK	64-23	2-0	Edwards (32)	Laimbeer (13)	G. Wilkins (24)
5-12	103-111	New York	64-24	2-1	Thomas (20)	Rodman (8)	Ewing (45)
5-13	102-90	New York	65-24	3-1	Edwards (19)	Rodman (14)	Ewing (30)
5-15	95-84	NEW YORK	66-24	4-1	Aguirre (25)	Rodman (11)	Ewing (22)

Eastern Conference finals: Pistons vs. Bulls

DATE	SCORE	OPPONENT	W-L	SERIES	TOP SCORER	TOP REBOUNDER	OPP. SCORER
5-20	86-77	CHICAGO	67-24	1-0	Dumars (27)	Rodman (13)	Jordan (34)
5-22	102-93	CHICAGO	68-24	2-0	Dumars (31)	Johnson, Laimbeer (8)	Jordan (20)
5-26	102-107	Chicago	68-25	2-1	Thomas (36)	Laimbeer (8)	Jordan (47)
5-28	101-108	Chicago	68-26	2-2	Thomas (26)	Rodman (20)	Jordan (42)
5-30	97-83	CHICAGO	69-26	3-2	Dumars (20)	Salley (10)	Jordan (22)
6-1	91-109	Chicago	69-27	3-3	Dumars (23)	Laimbeer, Rodman (8)	Jordan (29)
6-3	93-74	CHICAGO	70-27	4-3	Thomas (21)	Aguirre (10)	Jordan (31)

NBA Finals: Pistons vs. Trail Blazers

DATE	SCORE	OPPONENT	W-L	SERIES	TOP SCORER	TOP REBOUNDER	OPP. SCORER
6-5	105-99	PORTLAND	71-27	1-0	Thomas (33)	Laimbeer (15)	Drexler (21)
6-7	105-106	PORTLAND (OT)	71-28	1-1	Edwards, Laimbeer (26)	Laimbeer (11)	Drexler (33)
6-10	121-106	Portland	72-28	2-1	Dumars (33)	Laimbeer (12)	Kersey (27)
6-12	112-109	Portland	73-28	3-1	Thomas (32)	Laimbeer (12)	Drexler (34)
6-14	92-90	Portland	74-28	4-1	Thomas (29)	Laimbeer (17)	Duckworth, Porter (21)

HOW THEY FARED

Eastern Conference standings

CENTRAL	W-L	PCT	GB	HOME	ROAD	CONF
Detroit	59-23	.720	—	35-6	24-17	40-14
Chicago	55-27	.671	4	36-5	19-22	37-17
Milwaukee	44-38	.537	15	27-14	17-24	28-26
Cleveland	42-40	.512	17	27-14	15-26	30-24
Indiana	42-40	.512	17	28-13	14-27	30-24
Atlanta	41-41	.500	18	25-16	16-25	27-27
Orlando	18-64	.220	41	12-29	6-35	12-42

ATLANTIC	W-L	PCT	GB	HOME	ROAD	CONF
Philadelphia	53-29	.646	—	34-7	19-22	37-17
Boston	52-30	.634	1	30-11	22-19	36-18
New York	45-37	.549	8	29-12	16-25	30-24
Washington	31-51	.378	22	20-21	11-30	20-34
Miami	18-64	.220	35	11-30	7-34	11-43
New Jersey	17-65	.207	36	13-28	4-37	13-41

Western Conference standings

MIDWEST	W-L	PCT	GB	HOME	ROAD	CONF
San Antonio	56-26	.683	—	34-7	22-19	40-16
Utah	55-27	.671	1	36-5	19-22	38-16
Dallas	47-35	.573	9	30-11	17-24	29-27
Denver	43-39	.524	13	28-13	15-26	28-28
Houston	41-41	.500	15	31-10	10-31	28-28
Minnesota	22-60	.268	34	17-24	5-36	12-44
Charlotte	19-63	.232	37	13-28	6-35	13-43

PACIFIC	W-L	PCT	GB	HOME	ROAD	CONF
LA Lakers	63-19	.768	—	37-4	26-15	44-12
Portland	59-23	.720	4	35-6	24-17	41-15
Phoenix	54-28	.659	9	32-9	22-19	38-18
Seattle	41-41	.500	22	30-11	11-30	26-30
Golden State	37-45	.451	26	27-14	10-31	24-32
LA Clippers	30-52	.366	33	20-21	10-31	17-39
Sacramento	23-59	.280	40	16-25	7-34	14-42

Eastern Conference playoffs

FIRST ROUND

Detroit over Indiana, 3-0; Philadelphia over Cleveland, 3-2; Chicago over Milwaukee, 3-1; New York over Boston, 3-2.

SEMIFINALS

Detroit over New York, 4-1; Chicago over Philadelphia, 4-1.

FINALS

Detroit over Chicago, 4-3.

Western Conference playoffs

FIRST ROUND

Los Angeles Lakers over Houston, 3-1; San Antonio over Denver, 3-0; Portland over Dallas, 3-0; Phoenix over Utah, 3-2.

SEMIFINALS

Phoenix over Los Angeles Lakers, 4-1; Portland over San Antonio, 4-3.

FINALS

Portland over Phoenix, 4-2.

NBA Finals

Detroit over Portland, 4-1.

Pistons regular-season statistics (59-23)

PLAYER	G	MIN	FG-FGA	FG%	FT-FTA	FT%	REB	AST	PTS
Isiah Thomas	81	37.0	579-1322	.438	292-377	.775	3.8	9.4	18.4
Joe Dumars	75	34.4	508-1058	.480	297-330	.900	2.8	4.9	17.8
James Edwards	82	27.8	462-928	.498	265-354	.749	4.2	0.8	14.5
Mark Aguirre	78	25.7	438-898	.488	192-254	.756	3.9	1.9	14.1
Bill Laimbeer	81	33.0	380-785	.484	164-192	.854	9.6	2.1	12.1
Vinnie Johnson	82	24.0	334-775	.431	131-196	.668	3.1	3.1	9.8
Dennis Rodman	82	29.0	288-496	.581	142-217	.654	9.7	0.9	8.8
John Salley	82	23.3	209-408	.512	174-244	.713	5.4	0.8	7.2
William Bedford	42	5.9	54-125	.432	9-22	.409	1.4	0.1	2.8
Gerald Henderson	57	8.1	53-109	.486	12-15	.800	0.8	1.3	2.4
*Gerald Henderson	46	7.3	42-83	.506	10-13	.769	0.7	1.3	2.3
David Greenwood	37	5.5	22-52	.423	16-29	.552	2.1	0.3	1.6
Stan Kimbrough	10	5.0	7-16	.438	2-2	1.000	0.7	0.5	1.6
Scott Hastings	40	4.2	10-33	.303	19-22	.864	0.8	0.2	1.1
Ralph Lewis	4	1.5	0-1	.000	0-0	.000	0.0	0.0	0.0
TOTALS	82	—	3333-6980	.478	1713-2252	.761	44.4	24.3	104.3
OPPONENTS	82	—	3043-6809	.447	1785-2342	.762	40.5	21.5	98.3

Three-point goals: *Henderson 14-31 (.452), Henderson 17-38 (.447), Dumars 22-55 (.400), Laimbeer 57-158 (.361), Aguirre 31-93 (.333), Thomas 42-136 (.309), Hastings 3-12 (.250), Salley 1-4 (.250), Bedford 1-6 (.167), Johnson 5-34 (.147), Rodman 1-9 (.111), Edwards 0-3 (.000). Totals: 177-541 (.327). Opponents: 186-558 (.333).

* Totals with Detroit

Pistons playoff statistics (15-5)

PLAYER	G	MIN	FG-FGA	FG%	FT-FTA	FT%	REB	AST	PTS
Isiah Thomas	20	37.9	148-320	.463	81-102	.794	5.5	8.2	20.5
Joe Dumars	20	37.7	130-284	.458	99-113	.876	2.2	4.8	18.2
James Edwards	20	26.8	114-231	.494	58-96	.604	3.6	0.7	14.3
Bill Laimbeer	20	33.4	91-199	.457	25-29	.862	10.6	1.4	11.1
Mark Aguirre	20	22.0	86-184	.467	39-52	.750	4.6	1.4	11.0
Vinnie Johnson	20	23.2	85-184	.462	34-43	.791	2.8	2.7	10.3
John Salley	20	27.4	58-122	.475	74-98	.755	5.9	1.0	9.5
Dennis Rodman	19	30.5	54-95	.568	18-35	.514	8.5	0.9	6.6
David Greenwood	5	9.4	2-4	.500	1-4	.250	1.8	0.0	1.0
William Bedford	5	3.8	1-6	.167	2-2	1.00	0.4	0.0	0.8
Scott Hastings	5	3.2	1-4	.250	0-0	.000	0.0	0.0	0.4
Gerald Henderson	8	2.3	1-5	.200	0-0	.000	0.4	0.5	0.3
TOTALS	20	—	771-1638	.471	431-574	.751	43.7	21.1	101.8
OPPONENTS	20	—	698-1604	.435	449-570	.788	39.4	20.5	94.8

Three-point goals: Thomas 32-68 (.471), Laimbeer 15-44 (.341), Aguirre 8-24 (.333), Johnson 2-7 (.286), Dumars 5-19 (.263), Hastings 0-3 (.000), Henderson 0-3 (.000). Totals: 62-168 (.369). Opponents: 50-183 (.273).

PHOTO CREDITS

William Archie: 9, 15, 16, 17, 18, 19R, 20, 29, 30, 34, 54, 57B, 66, 67B, 69, 70, 79, 80T, 80B, 88T, 93R, 99, 101, 106, 107.

John Collier: 4, 5.

Manny Crisostomo: 91R, 92R.

William DeKay: 2, 31, back cover.

Hugh Grannum: 48.

Jessica Greene: 72L.

Daymon J. Hartley: 25, 104L.

Al Kamuda: 8, 14, 22, 24, 26, 27R, 28, 33, 37, 45, 53B, 56, 64B, 68.

Richard Lee: 6.

Pauline Lubens: 3, 10, 11T, 11B, 27T, 32, 35, 36, 38, 39, 40, 42, 50, 52, 59, 60, 64T, 73B.

John Luke: 21.

Craig Porter: Front cover, 1, 43R, 46, 47, 58, 62T, 62B, 65, 72T, 74, 75, 76, 77, 78T, 78B, 81R, 82, 83R, 86, 87, 88L, 89R, 90, 93L, 97, 98, 100, 102, 103R, 104T, 105R, 112.

Mary Schroeder: 12T, 12B, 13R, 51, 84L, 84T, 85R.

John A. Stano: 96, 103T.

George Waldman: 44.

KEY: T—top; B—bottom; R—right; L—left.